The
BEST of
DECORATIVE
PAINTING

The Best of Decorative Painting

EDITED BY GREG ALBERT
AND JENNIFER LONG

NORTH LIGHT BOOKS
CINCINNATI, OHIO

ABOUT THE EDITORS

Jennifer Long is Associate Editor for North Light Books. She received her Bachelor of Fine Arts in creative writing, with a minor in art, from Bowling Green State University. She paints in both acrylic and watercolor in her spare time.

Greg Albert is the Editorial Director of North Light Books. He has a formal art education and paints in various mediums. He also teaches evening classes in drawing and painting.

The Best of Decorative Painting. Copyright © 1998 by North Light Books. Manufactured in China. All rights reserved. No part of this book may be reproduced in any form or by any electronic or mechanical means including information storage and retrieval systems without permission in writing from the publisher, except by a reviewer, who may quote brief passages in a review. Published by North Light Books, an imprint of F&W Publications, Inc., 1507 Dana Avenue, Cincinnati, Ohio 45207. (800) 289-0963. First edition.

Other fine North Light Books are available from your local bookstore, art supply store or direct from the publisher.

02 01 00 99 98   5 4 3 2 1

Library of Congress Cataloging-in-Publication Data

The best of decorative painting / edited by Jennifer Long and Greg Albert.
     p.   cm.
Includes index.
ISBN 0-89134-905-7 (alk. paper)
1. Painting—Technique. 2. Decoration and ornament. I. Long, Jennifer. II. Albert, Greg.
TT385.B48   1998
745.7′23—dc21   98-12190
                                                         CIP

Production edited by Patrick Souhan
Cover designed by Mary Barnes-Clark
Interior designed by Clare Finney
Strokework borders created by Deanne Fortnam, MDA
Detail of *Roses*, cover and page 2 by Donna Bryant Waterson
Roses on pages 4 and 5 by Priscilla Hauser, MDA

ACKNOWLEDGMENTS

The editors wish to thank the artists who chose to share their work with others by contributing to this book. There is a great tradition among decorative artists to share their work, their time and their talents with others. This book would not have been possible without their generous cooperation. We also wish to thank our panel of judges for their help in selecting the pieces for this book: Anne Hevener, editor of *Decorative Artist's Workbook* magazine; Amy Leibrock, former managing editor of *Decorative Artist's Workbook*; Kathy Kipp, editor for North Light Books' decorative painting titles; and Heather Dakota, editor of Decorative Artist's Book Club. A big thank-you also goes to Jane Friedman for her invaluable help and even more invaluable humor during an endless summer of photo shoots.

Contents

Introduction ❧ *page 9*

1

BREATHTAKING FLORALS *page 10*

2

LUSCIOUS FRUIT
page 50

3

REALISTIC STILL LIFE *page 66*

4

HEARTWARMING SCENES *page 80*

5 COLORFUL WILDLIFE *page 90*

6 EXPRESSIVE PORTRAITS
page 104

7 TRADITIONAL STROKEWORK
page 114

Contributors ❧ page 140

8 CHRISTMAS CHEER
page 126

Pat Virch, *Company
Coming Serving Plate*,
acrylic on wooden plate,
16″ (41cm) diameter with
a 2″ (5cm) rim

Introduction

Decorative painting, as the pages of this book will show, is a rich and varied art form. With roots deep in many painting traditions—tole painting, folk art, traditional craftsmen's decoration and more—it has maintained a link with its origins in the utilitarian surfaces many decorative artists choose to paint on. From small furniture, frames, chests and boxes, to barrel staves, saw blades and sleds, all of these things were meant for other uses, but have been transformed by decorative artists into so much more.

This transformation is the very wonder of decorative painting. It is about making common objects into treasured things of beauty and reveals the timeless urge felt by humankind to enhance and enrich life by decoration. It is a statement of hope and optimism when the decorative artist takes an otherwise plain, everyday object and elevates it to art with a brush, paint, love, patience and skill.

This book is by no means an exhaustive survey, but it is truly representative of the high quality of decorative art being created today. Because of the often ordinary, even humble, nature of the surfaces and objects upon which decorative painting has been applied, decorative art has been too often overlooked. This book should dispel any notion that decorative painting should take second place to other popular art forms.

It is hoped that this volume will give decorative painting today a vast international audience. That those not aware of its richness, color and beauty will see how appealing this art form really is.

Most of the artists represented in this book are not the product of formal art school training. Many are self-taught, but all are fully trained and motivated by a passion for their art. This book is replete with examples of the superb quality they have achieved.

Decorative painting today is largely the result of a revival of traditional painting and folk art forms. More than a mere revival, it is a rebirth that occurred in the American heartland a quarter of a century ago. Old art forms were rescued from oblivion and renewed. New forms, inspired by the old, developed and grew.

In the early 1970s a group of decorative painting enthusiasts and teachers formed what was to become the Society of Decorative Painters. The Society has grown into a nationwide organization with members all across North America and in many foreign countries. The Society makes it possible for contemporary decorative painters to share their ever-growing knowledge, skills and techniques with countless students; to raise the awareness of decorative painting as an art form to a greater level; and to encourage high professional standards among decorative artists.

The key to the success of the Society is its commitment to sharing the joys of decorative painting with as many as possible by teaching others to know and appreciate the beauty and vitality of decorative painting, and by passing on the skills and training to artists everywhere. For more information, contact The Society of Decorative Painters, 393 N. McLean Blvd., Wichita, KS 67203-5968.

We hope you enjoy the many beautiful examples of decorative painting in this book, and that you take away a new appreciation of how this art form can enhance the quality of life for all of us.

Deanne Fortnam, MDA, *Clematis and Yellow Roses,* acrylic on wooden jewelry box, 18¼″ × 11″ × 5¼″ (46cm × 28cm × 13cm)

BREATHTAKING FLORALS

lowers are the most popular subject for decorative painters. The beautiful colors, delicate structure and almost endless variety of shapes have attracted artists for centuries.

Painting blooms and blossoms has always given decorative painters the opportunity to reflect on nature's great handiwork of field and garden, and to bring a bit of natural beauty into the daily lives of others.

The works in this chapter reveal the tremendous range of styles and approaches decorative artists bring to the subject. These painters strive in whatever medium they prefer—acrylics, oils, watercolors—to immortalize a fleeting moment of beauty.

DEANNE FORTNAM, MDA

I enjoy photographing the flowers in my gardens. During our bleak New England winters, the photos are a wonderful reminder that spring and summer will come again.

It was a happy discovery to find that the pink tones on these yellow roses coordinate with the pinks in the center vein areas of the clematis blossoms. Carrying these same colors on both flower forms helps to create harmony in the design. By including the same pinks as accent tones on the leaves, the entire painting becomes a coherent and pleasing visual image. I basecoated the top of the lid and the sides of the box with Dove Grey, then created a blended background by working

DecoArt Americana Raw Umber, Light Buttermilk and Taupe into the wet Dove Grey with a ¾-inch (19mm) filbert mop.

I created value scales on my palette for each main color in the design, then painted the leaves, clematis and finally the roses. After all the design elements were completed, I balanced the painting by carrying the palette colors throughout the design. I finished the piece by smoking the sides of the box and gold leafing the edge of the lid and ball feet.

Deanne Fortnam, MDA, *Clematis and Yellow Roses*, acrylic on wooden jewelry box, 18¼″ × 11″ × 5¼″ (46cm × 28cm × 13cm)

PAT WAKEFIELD, MDA

I enjoy painting in a photo-realistic style, including as much detail as possible. I must have the object I'm painting available; if I rely only on my memory, I might miss something. I prefer tube oils to achieve a rich color and smooth blend. I first rolled on two coats of black acrylic with a small paint roller to give some tooth to the smooth, slick surface of the board. After sanding lightly, I painted the background. I allowed this to dry before I transferred my drawing to the surface. Next, I painted the flowers and leaves and allowed them to dry, then layered the glass vase over them. My typical method for painting clear glass is: (1) paint what is behind the glass, (2) paint the back side of the glass, (3) paint what is inside the glass and (4) paint the front side of the glass. When the painting was completely dry I protected it with a good varnish made for oil paintings.

Pat Wakefield, MDA, *Iris Still Life*, oil on pressed board, 11″×17″ (28cm×43cm)

ENID HOESSINGER, CDA

This eight-sided box allowed me to paint a different flower and its meaning on each panel. I always carry a tiny booklet containing the symbolic meaning of different flowers—Victorians frequently used these floral symbols in bouquets to express their sentiments. Along with the roses on top, the box makes up a "bouquet" whose message is "An offering with *our love*, *His love*, that your *faith* and the *hope* of your loved ones will *endure*, that you may enjoy health, to live a life of *variety*, with *good education*, in *truth* and *agreement*, to find your own *True Love*." (J.H.H. 1997) I used DecoArt Americana Antique Teal for the background. This dark color allowed me to create good depth in the foliage and gave me an opportunity to push some flowers into the distance, creating dimension. The flowers were painted with black, white, blue-green, True Blue, Enid's Collection Brilliant Red, Antique Gold Deep and Yellow Light. I used no complex color mixing in this piece, opting instead for triple-loaded foliage and double-loaded flowers. I trimmed the edges with Glorious Gold and sealed the piece with acrylic spray.

Enid Hoessinger, CDA, *Say it With Flowers*, acrylic on wooden octagonal box, 9″ (23cm) diameter × 6″ (15cm) height

GINGER EDWARDS

Several years ago I bought a number of old books that looked like they needed a good home. Before long, I was eyeing them as surfaces to embellish with my decorative painting. Later, when I happened upon this wonderful Emily Post book with the "latest" in perfect manners (from the late 1930s and early 1940s), the first thing I thought of was a white rose—the epitome of perfection. I wanted to use the cover of the book just as it was, so I merely misted it lightly with a matte acrylic spray for protection. I used a palette knife to mix Titanium White and a speck of Yellow Ochre Light to create the basic white. Next I side loaded a rather large flat brush with Indigo and then generously loaded the opposite side of the brush with the white mix. Using a blending medium, I painted the rose with the side-loaded brush and a wet-on-wet technique. Once the rose was completed, I immediately sprayed it with matte acrylic spray to force-dry the painting. I then lightly tinted

the throat of the flower using the blending medium and tiny amounts of Yellow Ochre Light and Raw Sienna. I painted the leaves using a wet-on-wet technique and a blending medium, using a range of green mixtures from Greenish Umber plus a tiny amount of Indigo to Titanium White plus a small amount of Cadmium Yellow Light and a speck of Greenish Umber. When finished, I misted the leaves with the matte acrylic spray to force-dry them, then added tints of Raw Sienna to a few. As a final touch, I added dewdrops to the leaves and petals with a liner brush, then placed tints of Indigo and the basic white mixture behind the rose, using very small amounts of paint to keep the background color from overwhelming the painting.

Ginger Edwards, *Old Fashioned Elegance*, oil on book cover, 6″ × 9″ × 2″ (15cm × 23cm × 5cm)

PEGGI SEVERINI, CDA

In this design I wanted to show all the phases of the columbine flower, from bud formation to a fully opened blossom. Of course, it was also important to turn this study into a decorative piece. The Colorado native columbine (our state flower) is blue and white with yellow stamens, so the color scheme was a natural. I decided to use an antique-looking lacy background to enhance the flowers' delicate appearance. I first basecoated the plate with a pale blue acrylic, then glued a piece of lace over the plate with a moveable adhesive. Next, I spray painted the background through the lace with a medium blue acrylic. The lace acted as a mask; when it was removed, it left a pale blue lace pattern showing through the medium blue background. My students discovered an interesting variation while working with the lace mask: If you neglect to glue the lace

down tightly before spraying it, the edges of the painted lace pattern take on a soft, fuzzy appearance, creating a pleasing effect. After spraying the piece with Krylon Matte 1311 to seal it, I applied the columbine pattern and began painting the design in oils, starting with three midrange values. When these areas were dry, I came back and added highlights and the deeper shadows needed to create dimension. When the entire design was dry, I varnished the whole piece with a matte brush-on varnish. Later a soft luster was added by buffing the plate with wax.

Peggi Severini, CDA, *Columbines and Old Lace,* oil over acrylic background on wooden plate, 10″ (25cm) diameter

ARLENE BECK, MDA

I loved this piece as soon as I saw it. It's functional, but when not in use, it folds and can be used as an accent piece. I can visualize it among silver, soft reflective lights and, naturally, a fresh bouquet of pink roses. Imagine it sitting in a feminine room next to a fainting chair, in front of a fireplace, or in a rose- or garden-themed room. Although the size and shape of this surface lends itself to many subjects, florals are my favorite, so I chose a floral theme. Never one to shy away from the challenge of painting realistic detail, I was inspired by the ruffling sweet peas that grow in my garden and by the beautiful rose with the light center and dark edges. I finished the piece with an acrylic spray varnish.

Arlene Beck, MDA, *Sunlit Roses,* acrylic on wooden folding table, 15″×25″ (38cm×64cm)

DOLORES LENNON, MDA

Roses are strong, yet delicate, graceful in appearance and nurturing to the spirit. These roses were created and named for Alaina Lepper—soon to be married to my son Matt—who embodies all of these qualities, as a nurse and as a woman. Many of us are fortunate in knowing someone who makes us smile just to hear his or her name spoken. Alaina is such a person. I paid special attention to realism in painting these roses. The background of the box is painted with a soft hush of blended colors, done specifically to soften and settle the roses into the surface. To complete this loving keepsake box, I trimmed the sides and inside of the box with lace and ribbon.

Dolores Lennon, MDA, *Alaina's Roses*, oil on wooden box,
10½″ × 7½″ × 7″ (27cm × 19cm × 18cm)

ANDY B. JONES, CDA

I painted this orchid in hopes of creating a painting with a pastel and frosted appearance. I used tube acrylics in a dry-brush technique, where layers of opaque colors are optically blended. I stenciled the background through a piece of lace, adding to the delicate appearance of the flower. The handmade watercolor paper framed in a shadowbox was a departure from painting on a functional surface, and I think fitting for this piece.

Andy B. Jones, CDA, *Single Orchid,* acrylic on watercolor paper, 11″×14″ (28cm×36cm)

CINDY FORSYTHE, MDA

This hanging tool chest was very appealing to me the minute I saw it at the wood shop. My husband had constantly been accusing me or our children of taking his tools and never putting them back in the garage. Well, let me tell you, he really never looked beyond his nose, because nearly every time I went to look for myself, there was the "missing" tool, almost in plain sight!

I knew I wanted to hang this piece in my kitchen, but I didn't want a fruit design. I photographed this hibiscus on one of our many trips to Hawaii. I first sealed the box surface with a wood sealer, then stained the inside, outside edge and back with a mixture of Burnt Umber and Odorless Turpenoid. I painted the background with a neutral acrylic color, allowing the focus to be totally on the flower. I lightly sprayed the dry background with Krylon Matte 1311 before transferring the pattern on. I painted wet-into-wet, giving me time to blend or wipe out what I didn't like. I used the chisel edge of the brush with white and reds to get the veining effect of the flower. I painted the leaves with mixes of black and Cadmium Yellow Light, and black and Cadmium Yellow Medium, then tinted them with the reds from the flowers. I added the filler flowers to provide contrast and more color. I went back and glazed weaker areas using a glazing medium. When the painting was dry, I covered it with a good varnish and waxed the entire surface, resulting in a beautiful, smooth finish.

Cindy Forsythe, MDA, *Ladies Hanging Tool Chest With Hibiscus*, oil on wooden tool chest, 12″ × 15½″ × 2½″ (30cm × 39cm × 6.3cm)

JACKIE SHAW

My paintings usually contain bits of sentiment or symbolism relevant to my family. If the painting is for a friend or is a commissioned piece, I try to work in symbolism that would be appropriate for the recipient. The painting on this bentwood museum box is no exception. The large rose at the base represents my beloved husband, the anchor of our family. The three full roses in the middle are our three daughters, two of whom are joined by their husbands, represented by the large buds. Our youngest daughter, not married at the time of the painting, was dating a young man we were not fond of, so you notice that the bud near her rose is fading out of the picture. (And he did! He was later replaced by a super young man, our third son-in-law). The two small buds are our two grandchildren by our eldest daughter and son-in-law. There should now be three more tiny buds added, but that's another painting! I am the rose up top, heading out into left field where my super supportive family knows they can always find me, doing "my thing." I did the painting with Loew-Cornell synthetic Taklon brushes and DecoArt acrylic paints in a variety of greens and pinks, using multiple layers of fine washes, meticuously built up. I scumbled on the background for the roses with a variety of greens. Gold leaf framing trims the roses—I laid it on a dull red background. I depicted a scroll border along one side of the gold leaf by outlining and shading it with brown tones. I loosely painted the flower border on the side of the lid to provide contrast to the detailed roses and leaves on top. After decorating the side, I sponged and spattered it to further subdue the painting. Strokework, my foremost painting love, embellishes the side of the box and creates a border for a favorite quote which succinctly expresses my optimistic approach to life: *Do not complain that the rosebush has thorns, but rejoice, instead, that it has roses.* (Author unknown.)

Jackie Shaw, *A Family of Love,* acrylic and gold leaf on bentwood box, 13″ × 18″ × 9″ (33cm × 46cm × 23cm)

JEANIE T. GROVES, CDA

This pillow top, with its warm spring colors, would look lovely tucked into a wicker chair in a sunroom. The warm colors of the flower can easily be altered to cooler tones to fit other color schemes. The traditional silk dye colors are vibrant and transparent, allowing the beauty of the silk fabric to show in the finished pillow. Before the pillow was sewn, I painted the white silk with jacquard traditional silk dyes. I used clear water base resist to outline the design, stripe and border. When the resist was dry, I painted the flower and leaves with a wet-on-wet technique. When the leaves were completely dry, I detailed

the vein lines very lightly with a red fabric pen. I lightly salted the background area and the border with silk salt and kosher salt while the dyes in these areas were wet. The salt created texture in the background and border, producing a nice contrast to the smoothness of the flowers and leaves. After the dyes were set, I sewed the pillow top onto a backing of white silk to complete the pillowcase.

Jeanie T. Groves, CDA, *Summer Splendor Pillow Top*, traditional silk dye on 8mm silk fabric, 18″ × 18″ (46cm × 46cm)

MARY L. BEAN

Mama always planted sweet peas in the spring. They were such a joyful jumble of color that I still smile and remember my childhood when I see sweet peas today. I tried to capture this feeling of fun in my painting. After masking out the flowers and buds, I used a wet-on-wet technique for the background, adding salt to create texture. I painted the flowers with warm and cool reds, blues and yellows, varying them in intensity and combinations to give a multitude of colors. I then added details and used negative painting in order to strengthen the background and give contrast where needed. I used glazing to adjust some areas of the painting. For these techniques I used a 1-inch (25mm) aquarelle brush, a no. 6 and no. 12 round and a no. 1 liner. I love the color, design and spontaneity of watercolor. I find the process and transparent characteristics of the medium to be a pleasant challenge.

Mary L. Bean, *Sweet Peas,* watercolor on Arches 140 lb. cold-pressed watercolor paper, 11″ × 15″ (28cm × 38cm)

TRUDY BEARD, CDA

This nostalgic scene, surrounded by tulips, reflects wonderful childhood memories of a favorite aunt. I can still picture her wearing a wide-brimmed straw hat while tending to her pansies and tulips. I painted the box inside and out with acrylic paint, except for the vingnette which I based with white gesso. The small landscape was painted first. In painting this scene, I wanted to create a feeling of distance and atmosphere; therefore, I used color values in the light to middle range. In addition, I painted very little texture into the trees and fields—this also adds to the distant look. When I painted the tulips, leaves and lilacs, I painted with more contrast, used stronger

values and added more details. I did the entire piece with a wet-on-wet technique, blocking in values then softly blending. I added highlights and accents last. Note that all of the elements in the design have been accented with values of the blue sky colors. To finish the piece, with the design protected, I antiqued the box and then flecked it with mixtures of colors from my palette.

Trudy Beard, CDA, *Aunt Ida's Tulips*, oil on wooden flower box, 13″×8½″×7″ (33cm×22cm×18cm)

PRISCILLA HAUSER, MDA

One day I was in a stationery store and found a box of handmade paper, into which beautiful flower petals had been pressed. I bought the box and wrote a letter to the manufacturer. Much to my joy, I received a reply and was able to purchase this elegant paper in large sheets. It was this soft paper, full of flower petals, that inspired my painting, *A Celebration of Roses*. This painting could be created in any medium desired. I chose oils. After drawing the design onto paper, I basecoated or undercoated the design with Resin Gel and let it dry. This sealed and filled the porous paper. Next, using my basic brushstroke, dry-brush blend leaf technique, I created the leaves in dark, medium and light values and finally the beautiful roses in different values of pink and burgundy. I would love to teach you to paint roses in my seminars or through the pages of my many books, which can be found in art and craft stores around the world.

Priscilla Hauser, MDA, *A Celebration of Roses*, oil on handmade flower petal paper, 24″ × 18″ (70cm × 45.7cm)

SUE PRUETT, MDA

I designed this piece for my teaching tour in Japan, where I had been requested to do a rose in a clear glass vase. I bought the vase at an antique store while attending a seminar at Cheri Rol's studio. Cheri helped me design the wood piece, so I have named this design after her. At home, I set up and photographed the vase and rose, then painted from the photographs. I used a black-and-white photocopy of one of the photos to help me see the dark and light values. I basecoated the rose and leaves with solid coverage, then moistened the areas with extender. Using a wet-on-wet blending technique, I built the values up, working each value within a smaller area than the one previous. I did the glass vase with transparent values of light and dark, building and pyramiding until I reached the final "glint" of light. This is a great study in creating realism, both in the rose and in the different planes of the vase.

Sue Pruett, MDA, *Cheri's Rose*, acrylic on wooden necklace holder, 12″ × 16″ (30cm × 41cm)

PAT PARKER

Spring is an especially joyful time here in upstate New York. After months and months of short days, long, cold nights, snowstorms and ice storms, the first signs of spring are like a saving grace! When the snow finally melts and the days lengthen, the little white crocuses poke their heads through the ground, followed soon after by daffodils and early tulips. These first flowers brave the dangers of snow, ice and frost to renew our faith. The world has come alive again! While painting and teaching another decorative artist's "spring" floral wreath—which included roses, lilies and geraniums—I got to thinking about how all those flowers were actually summer flowers where I live. I decided to design a new wreath to celebrate the first brave flowers of the Northeastern spring.

Together, my class and I discussed which flowers we loved most in the early spring. Later I sat down with photographs and seed catalogs to draw them. I put these blooms together with a beautiful Mint Julep picot ribbon and bow, drawn from my imagination. This wreath is my favorite design, reflecting my love of early spring flowers.

Pat Parker, *Spring Floral Wreath*, acrylic on wooden wreath, 21" (53cm) diameter

DOXIE KELLER

I have always wanted to paint in pastel colors. I found this very difficult until DecoArt developed their waterbased, transparent Heavenly Hues paints. These colors are easily blended or mixed to create a wider array of colors. They can be used for glazing, staining and transparent coverage, and are wipable or removable for forty-eight to seventy-two hours, making the paints easy for beginners to use. I created the dimensional floral design freehand using a two- to three-inch flexible palette knife and decorating paste, which is similar in texture and thickness to canned or royal cake frosting. I like to tell my students to think "peanut butter sandwich" when laying down the decorating paste.

Doxie Keller, *Pastel Dimensional Flowers—Easy Does It*, DecoArt Decorating Paste and Heavenly Hues paint on wooden Bombay box, 19″ × 13″ × 13″ (48cm × 33cm × 33cm)

DONNA BRYANT WATERSON

Whether painting on canvas, fabric or furniture, roses have an undeniable, universal appeal. They are by far my favorite subject to paint. Since I prefer to start on a colored background instead of white canvas, I applied several coats of gesso, then toned my canvas with an acrylic color in a midvalue range of the primary hue used in my painting. I painted the design in stages, allowing each stage to dry completely before the next was added. Using a drying medium is invaluable with my

painting techniques. There's a bittersweet blend of exhilaration and sadness when a painting is completed. It's like a wonderful vacation: You're glad to be back, but you'll miss the joy and excitement of your travels.

Donna Bryant Waterson, *Roses*, oil on canvas, 16″ × 20″ (41cm × 51cm) oval

JACKIE O'KEEFE

This unusual piece of tin is a reproduction of an Early American document box, handmade by tinsmiths to store important papers like wedding and birth certificates, mortgages and other legal forms. Back in the days before safe deposit boxes or climate-controlled banks, it was necessary to protect precious things, not just from theft, but also from bugs, rodents and weather. I purchased this box already prepared with a black primer so it was only necessary to basecoat it with a spray matte acrylic paint. After transferring the details of the design

to the box with a stylus and white graphite, I painted it using multiple layers of acrylic paints. By personalizing the banner, I created a family heirloom that will be passed down through other generations of our family. I finished the piece with a spray matte acrylic varnish.

Jackie O'Keefe, *Family Records*, acrylic on tin document box, 10" × 7" × 6" (25cm × 18cm × 15cm)

DONNA DEWBERRY

When I began painting, the one thing I most wanted to paint was a rose. I would sit down at my kitchen table in the evening and practice, practice, practice. There were times when painting a rose seemed an unattainable task. I don't think I can describe just how excited I was the evening (actually it was the wee hours of the morning) I painted what I considered to be an acceptable version of a rose. Soon I was painting roses on everything in sight. However, even if I had never painted anything again after that evening, I would have been satisfied.

After viewing my in-law's collection of roses, I was inspired to paint these multicolored roses. The lighter shades of leaves in the background and on the edges were achieved using water sparingly to create a watercolor effect that embellishes the tray without taking away from the roses. The small filler flowers are simply painted with a C-stroke. The centers are dotted in with the handle of the brush. The roses themselves are painted entirely using the One-Stroke technique, as was the foliage surrounding the roses. Once you try this technique, I think you'll agree that painting roses can be fun. Those ever mysterious, precisely beautiful, elegantly constructed representations of Mother Nature are attainable. I hope painting them brings as much joy to you as it does to me.

Donna Dewberry, *Rose Bouquet Serving Tray*, FolkArt acrylics on wood, 18″×12″×3″ (45.7cm×30.5cm×7.6cm)

PHILLIP C. MYER

I first pickled the wooden stationery box with an acrylic white-wash to provide a light background for the rose painting. I marbleized the surrounding sides of the box in a Rose Aurora colored marble pattern, using newspaper, feathers and soft blending brushes to create the illusion. I placed a matching inset border of marble on the top panel. I wanted to frame the rose design with a mat-like shape: I love the look of well-placed design elements that produce a very striking graphic impact.

After completing the background and trim elements, I sealed the entire surface with waterbased polyurethane varnish to protect the finished areas while working on the rose painting. I painted the leaves, rose and buds in acrylic, using a combination of wet-into-wet, side-loading and dry-brush painting techniques: I like to start my acrylic painting with an opaque basecoat, then develop light, medium and dark values in a wet-into-wet blending technique, working very quickly. This establishes a section of the painting at a time very effectively.

When all areas are dry, I go back and redefine, sharpen and clean up the quickly blended areas using a side-loading technique. I add more shading or highlighting and accents with a properly side-loaded flat brush. Finally, I lightly stroke on additional highlights and accents with a dry-brush technique. I love to finish my work with six to seven coats of waterbased polyurethane varnish, wet sanding between every three coats for a smooth, beautiful finish.

Phillip C. Myer, *A Blooming Rose*, acrylic on stationery box, 10″ × 13″ × 5″ (25cm × 33cm × 13cm)

HELEN STADTER, MDA

This project came to be because birdhouses are very popular now and I enjoy using them as decorations in my own home. Flowers have always been one of my favorite things to paint—especially roses, whether they are stroke roses or are painted petal by petal. I painted these wild roses petal by petal in shades of pink and rose. I added some muting and flyspecking to the edges using the rose colors to create interest and enhance the overall painting.

Helen Stadter, MDA, *Roses Run Wild*, acrylic on wooden birdhouse, 6″×7″×6″ (15cm×18cm×15cm)

COLLEEN UNDERWOOD, CDA

I designed this piece for my mother's seventy-fifth birthday. Her love of roses made the painting a natural choice, and I knew she would get pleasure from seeing it hanging on her wall. I wanted to keep the piece soft and pastel in color. I chose a warm neutral background, which seemed a natural setting for the roses. I used a glazing technique to bring out the highlights, shading and detail. Then I roughed around the design to soften and enhance it. I trimmed the edges of the piece with gold leaf, then antiqued over this. I finished the piece with several coats of varnish.

Colleen Underwood, CDA, *Mother's Roses*, oil and gold leaf on wooden mirror, 10″×16″ (25cm×41cm)

JO ALLAN

After seeing a wall sconce decorated with bronzing powder poppies that I did at a convention, my students asked me to teach them the poppies on a wooden box. My husband designed the box and I took bits and pieces from the sconce design and added my own poppies for the lid. To create the bronzed flowers, I applied varnish to the area to be bronzed, then when it was just dry, I gently dusted on the bronzing powder with a soft brush. Go very lightly at first—the varnish will grab the gobs of powder if you overload the brush. I used four colors of Venus bronze powder on this project: Aluminum Powder, Patent Turkey Red, Vernis Martin Gold and Pure Metal Leaf Palegold. Always wear a mask when using bronzing powder so you don't inhale any of the dust. I mixed the powders with varnish to do the liner work. After the bronzing work had dried, I gave the entire piece two to three coats of varnish to protect the surface.

Jo Allan, *Bronze Poppies*, bronzing powder and varnish on a wooden box, 7″ × 10½″ × 10½″ (18cm × 27cm × 27cm)

BARBARA A. NEFF

Porcelain is a beautiful surface to paint. Most porcelain is paintable and needs little or no preparation. If it's rough, you need to sand it lightly, then clean off the dust and fingerprints with alcohol. I found this vase at an HIA show several years ago. Its height made it a perfect piece for an iris, my favorite flower.

I have loved beautiful flowers since I was a girl and would visit my grandmother, who had an old-fashioned flower garden with lots of irises. My mother also had a green thumb—but not I—so I just love to paint flowers. I draw my designs using photos or real flowers. I love the color of the Dark Night iris; it was a challenge to choose the colors that would re-create this flower. I basecoated the flower with the darkest value of purple mix, adding a light blue-violet to bring up the midvalue to the lightest highlight. I also added tints of Alizarin Crimson. After the design was dry, I went back and added extra shadowing and highlights as needed. When the final touches were dry, I used blending and glazing medium and soft, muted shades of the flower colors to paint the background of the vase. I used a mop brush to soften and blend the colors, giving the design a finished look. When the oils were dry, I sprayed the piece lightly with several coats of matte finish.

Barbara A. Neff, *Dark Night Iris*, oil and alkyd on porcelain vase, 13½″ × 5½″ (34cm × 14cm)

MARLENE BARKER, CDA

Spring comes late to the Colorado high country where I live. While I can't risk planting pansies in my garden until June, I can paint them in March when spring is far away and the snow is still falling—I have found this to be one of the greatest blessings in being a decorative artist. This lovely porcelain egg box was designed with just that in mind. The soft hues of spring made a perfect complement to the delicate porcelain. Porcelain is one of my favorite surfaces to paint on. Giving the piece a light spray of Krylon Matte 1311 before painting will keep the oil paint from soaking in too quickly. I did the background with a light coverage of the palette colors and allowed it to dry before starting the design. I used a large brush and a final dusting with a mop to keep the background

soft. When painting the flowers and ribbon, the paint application must be kept very light. The light and dark values can be strengthened in a second application using Winsor & Newton Blending and Glazing Medium, if necessary. As a final touch, after the leaves were dry I added the dewdrops, again using the glazing medium. This gives the piece the look of gentle spring rain. What could be more perfect than a touch of springtime to enjoy in the midst of winter?

Marlene Barker, CDA, *Springtime Blessings*, oil on porcelain egg box, 3½″ × 5″ × 3½″ (8.8cm × 13cm × 8.8cm)

CHARLES JOHNSON

I enjoy painting on oval or round boxes as they will always
be useful. This box is made by Designs by Bentwood in
Thomasville, Georgia. The top is an easy faux finish using
acrylic paints. The color is layered using crumpled paper towels
and veins are done with a liner brush. The bottom resembles
a drape of material tied on each end of the box with a bow
entwined with roses. The lace trim at the bottom overlaps a
crackle finish made with DecoArt Weathered Wood applied
over DecoArt Glorious Gold paint.

Charles Johnson, *Victorian Keepsake Box*, acrylic on wooden box,
8½″ × 15″ (22cm × 38cm)

AUDREY D. MITCHELL, CDA

The rose on this magazine holder is one I sketched from my backyard rose garden. I simply changed the color of the rose to match my family room decor. To prepare the surface, I first sealed the wood. I then stained the background with the same paint color I used on the trimwork in my family room, thinned to a glaze. I painted the rose one petal at a time, then went back and reinforced my lights and darks. I painted the leaves in the same manner, incorporating warm and cool greens and adding tints of the rose colors here and there. The entire painting was done in one sitting, blended wet-into-wet. When the painting was completely dry, I applied several coats of varnish, sanding lightly between each coat. To finish the wooden surface, I applied Goddard's Cabinet Maker's wax with grade 0000 steel wool, then polished it with a soft cloth. I gathered the side fabric (sewn from a bedsheet that matched the rose) onto half-inch dowels, inserted into the painted end boards.

Audrey D. Mitchell, CDA, *Blended Rose on Magazine Holder*, oil on wooden magazine holder 5½″ × 16½″ × 15¼″ (14cm × 42cm × 39cm)

AVIS BRAUN, CDA

Along with the first flowers of spring come the pussy willows across the road from my house. This was my inspiration for a design on a piece of wood I had purchased at a convention which I just *had* to have, but had no idea what I'd do with. I based the box with cool and warm neutral acrylics for a soft, delicate look, then painted the design in oils. I blended all the tulips with the chisel edge to give them more texture and interest. The upper right tulip is warmer than the other tulip, giving it more importance. I added tints and accents to the leaves and tulips as I painted them. When everything was dry, I rouged behind the design with a toned-down tulip color.

Avis Braun, CDA, *Tulip Time*, oil on wooden vanity, 9½″ × 8½″ × 5½″ (24cm × 22cm × 14cm)

PAT WAYMON

The special beauty of a peaceful spring garden leaves memories that last forever. Unfortunately, flowers don't last forever, but by painting each and every petal, you or someone you love can enjoy a beautiful painted garden for many years to come. There are so many flowers to pick from, but I do believe daisies are my favorite. I included poppies because they are such strong flowers, reminding me of the strength we all need to build character and to teach our families to work together. These flowers are the focal point of my painting, as my family is the focal point of my life. Lilacs not only are a joy to see and smell, they make great filler flowers. This watering can is perfect for use in the garden or for houseplants, or just to adorn your favorite room. I painted this piece with soft, tran-

quil colors that are pleasant to live with. You can tint the background to tie it in with the color scheme in your house. The design can be adjusted to fit many different surfaces from a chair cushion to a book cover. It could even be used as a border, pulling your whole room together. Or paint it as a special gift to share with someone you love. There is no limit to what you can paint. Be creative and doors will open for you. Look forward to new challenges, develop your skills and have fun with your painting. Happy painting!

Pat Waymon, *Spring*, oil on metal watering can, 12½″ × 16″ (32cm × 41cm)

JUDY DUARTE

Some time ago, I was asked to paint a piece for *Let's Paint* magazine. I discussed my project with Chuck from Wood Chuck, Inc. in Temecula, California, and we came up with this wonderful Victorian footstool. I love Victorian decor (and every other thing about that era). I decided to paint this piece to go in my own house; something I haven't done in a long time. The simple design lends itself well to the pastel color scheme. Soft, delicate and quietly elegant, this footstool fits beautifully into my living room decor. This is truly one of my favorite pieces and I'm glad to have the opportunity to share it with you.

Judy Duarte, *Victorian Footstool*, DecoArt acrylic paint on wooden stool, 12″×10″×11″ (30cm×25cm×28cm)

CAROL EMPET, CDA

When I first started to paint fourteen years ago, I wanted to paint everything. But somewhere along the line, flowers became the only thing I enjoyed painting, especially floral wooden cutouts on mirror frames, wreaths, door swags, cabinets and boxes. The combination of pansies, sweet William, daisies and zinnias in this design comes from my own garden; they are the first flowers I grew as a child and are still my favorites. The variety of petal configurations, overall shapes, textures and details of these four flowers, with the addition of serrated leaves, makes for an interesting and pleasing design. When painting flowers, I'm always searching for unusual color combinations, so to coordinate with the natural color of the basket, I chose a yellow-orange/blue-violet complementary color scheme. The white daisies are positioned to act as a "resting place" for the eye between the more vibrant colors. I first based the flowers with acrylics, then rubbed on shades, highlights, accents and tints with alkyds. I always pre-mix about five values, light to dark, of each color I'm using for painting the "body color," shades and highlights. I never use green paint straight from the bottle. Rather, I mix blues and yellows to make a variety of greens for my leaves, coordinating them with the temperature, intensity and values of the flowers. Being an avid gardener as well as a painter, I believe that to paint flowers, you have to know them intimately. May you always have beautiful flowers—real or painted—in your life.

Carol Empet, CDA, *Gathering Basket*, acrylic and alkyd on wooden cutout, 14″ × 8″ (36cm × 20cm)

ANN GRZYMSKI, CDA

Pansies stand for thoughts—thoughts of my grandmother's garden where the pansies were the first flowers she planted in early spring. Now pansies are usually the first flowers I paint in January, when no signs of spring have yet appeared in my part of the country. Their brightly colored faces are a joy to paint on cold, dreary days. To prepare the surface, I first stained the entire box. When dry, I painted only the top of the lid with Old Parchment acrylic paint. I then lightly sprayed the lid with Krylon Matte 1311 and transferred the design. Next, using a painting medium, I brush-mixed the paints to obtain subtle variations within the colors, which included Cadmium Yellow, Alizarin Crimson, Cadmium Red, Cadmium

Orange and black. I painted the leaves with mixes of Cinnabar Green Light, Prussian Blue, black, white and Cadmium Yellow. I did the forget-me-nots with mixes of Prussian Blue and white. To create harmony within the painting, I stroked a little of the flower colors onto the leaves. When the paint was dry, I antiqued the edge of the lid with Burnt Umber oil paint. Finally, I sprayed the entire box with Krylon Satin Finish varnish and glued on the lace.

Ann Grzymski, CDA, *Pansy Box*, oil and lace on bentwood box, 6″ × 2″ (15cm × 5cm)

JO AVIS MOORE, MDA

I collect plates with various fruits and flowers. I decided to use two of my favorites, roses and plums, for this design. I painted the entire background with a soft neutral gray. I painted the soft pink stroke roses first, then the plums and finally the leaves. I refined the painting several times, and added water droplets as a finishing touch. When painting a design like this, remember to tint your leaves and other elements with colors pulled from your center of interest. I used both warm and cool tints on the plums. After the design was finished, I chose a complementary wine color for the outer rim. On this I added a border of small, vein-like lines with tiny leaves and berries. I finished the piece with a spray satin varnish.

Jo Avis Moore, MDA, *A Plate With Roses and Plums,* oil over acrylic background on round wooden plate, 12″ (30cm) diameter

GLORIA PERKINS

I began my lifelong love of art as a child. I have taught oil painting for fifteen years, from local art classes to national conventions and travel teaching. While art is a great enjoyment for me, the greatest reward is seeing students complete a painting that is an expression of themselves. I prefer painting with oils, and although my paintings aren't limited in subject matter, I especially enjoy florals, particularly roses. The rose is the most beautiful, enchanting, romantic and challenging of all florals. *Grandmother's Roses* is done in an impressionistic style. The colors are intermingled all over the canvas to create a sense of unity. Temperature is very important, as is value change. By creating lost edges, I have achieved a three-dimensional effect on a flat surface. As I complete a painting, I want it to exude a special, energetic drama that sets it apart and conveys an emotion of freedom and color.

Gloria Perkins, *Grandmother's Roses*, oil on canvas, 20″ × 24″ (51cm × 61cm)

Mary McLean, CDA, *Glorious Fruit*, oil on wooden basket lid, 11″ (28cm) diameter × 4½″ (11.4cm) deep

LUSCIOUS FRUIT

Fruit, the child of the flower, has also attracted the decorative painter for countless generations. Fruit is a potent symbol. It can symbolize God's bounteous gifts to humankind, the promise of hope and life hidden in the seed it contains, or the satisfaction of a meal, especially shared with family and friends.

Fruit conjures up powerful memories of home and childhood. Who can forget the sweetness of an apple eaten on the way home from school, or the juicy taste of a pear snatched on the way out to play?

Fruit also reminds us of one essential ingredient in our lives—sunlight. Each piece of fruit contains the stored energy of the sun. Since light is an essential element of art as well, fruit is an obvious choice for the artist. How could anyone resist such a powerful symbol wrapped in such a delightful package?

MARY McLEAN, CDA

Fruit offers an endless array of luminous colors to feed the visual soul. I have always been attracted to the elegance of deep garnets, royal violets and majestic golds. The interplay of these colors in my design creates a vision of radiant gifts from nature. The control of color harmony in a painting always presents a special challenge. No color stands alone; visual perception is enhanced through the development of color relationships. As I progressed with the painting, new color assignments seemed to appear almost magically within the designated

areas . . . reds, yellows, oranges, garnet and blue-violets. These hues were repeated in various sizes and placements throughout the design. The blueberries introduced a repetitive cool element, creating variety in the otherwise unified warm tones of the painting.

Mary McLean, CDA, *Glorious Fruit*, oil on wooden basket lid, 11″ (28cm) diameter × 4½″ (11.4cm) deep

CAROLYN L. PHILLIPS

This beautiful apple-shaped wooden plate was the inspiration for this project. What could be more appropriate than apples—with a pear tossed in for a little variety? I basecoated the center area with off-white acrylic and applied a transparent stain to the rest of the surface with red-brown acrylic, thinned with clear glazing medium. I painted the edge of the plate and the routed bead trim with a rich gold metallic. I painted the design in a watercolor technique, using layers of very transparent washes and tints of acrylic color. I glazed warm, sunny colors onto the upper right, highlight areas of the background, gradually fading to cooler, more shady colors in the lower left areas. I applied clear glazing medium between some of the layers of color. I tinted the fruit, leaves and branches with transparent yellow, followed by washes of shading color to create form. I

allowed the pale background color to show through for the highlights, then brightened some with more opaque touches of yellow and white. I applied transparent blue "reflected light" to the lower left, shaded side of all objects. To finish the piece, I applied a coat of clear glazing medium to all surfaces, followed by four or five coats of waterbased acrylic varnish. To reduce the shine and harden the varnished surface, I squeezed a small amount of retarder onto the surface to act as a lubricant, then used a small square of nylon scrub pad to very lightly rub the surface. With a soft cloth, I wiped excess retarder from the surface and buffed it to a beautiful matte sheen.

*Carolyn L. Phillips, Apple and Pear Plate, acrylic on wooden plate, 12"
(30cm) diameter × ¾" (1.9cm) deep*

PEGGY NUTTALL

I have always admired beautiful, heirloom china plates. I was determined to see if I could come close to this effect using oils and alkyds on a wooden surface, which would be a big plus in my book since wooden plates are unbreakable. I started first with the sharper focus leaves using Olive Green and Sap Green, varying the highlights from leaf to leaf. Next I painted the apples, then the background using the two greens, Cadmium Yellow Light and white. The shadow leaves add depth and dimension to the plate. When I completed the painting,

I placed the plate where I could view it from time to time. Looking at it with a fresh eye enabled me to spot areas that needed more shadow leaves and strengthening of darks and lights. When satisfied with the end result, I applied three coats of waterbased varnish and lightly sanded the entire piece with fine steel wool.

Peggy Nuttall, *Spray of Apples*, alkyd on wooden plate, 11½″ (29cm) diameter

BRENDA STEWART, CDA

I developed *Nature's Bounty* in response to many student requests for an intensive study leaf workshop. In this instance, I allowed the subject matter to determine the color harmony. Once I decided to establish red as the predominant color family, the challenge was to pull the blueberries into the composition. This was done by painting them in purple-blues and tinting them heavily in reds. They are balanced in the overall project by the blues and purples in the blackberries, the blue-toned darks and blue tints of the leaves. Southern Louisiana humidity presents problems with drying time of an oil project. For that reason, when I wish to use oil techniques, I paint in alkyds. The techniques used for these two mediums are exactly the same, the alkyds simply set up and dry more rapidly. After applying a blending medium, I painted the leaves and fruit with a wet-in-wet technique. Since alkyds set up more rapidly than oils, I used a series of overpaintings to fully develop the project. To repeat both colors and subject matter, I painted a muted trim design of currants and leaves at the top of the chest. Before antiquing, the painting was allowed to dry, and I applied one coat of the finish varnish. I then antiqued the spice chest with an alkyd mixture to soften and mellow the overall composition.

Brenda Stewart, CDA, *Nature's Bounty Spice Chest*, alkyd on wooden spice chest, 13″ × 16″ × 5¼″ (33cm × 41cm × 13cm)

MARY JANE TODD, CDA

I painted this design on an old salad bowl I found at a garage sale. This design can be reduced or enlarged to fit any size bowl you have. Before painting a wooden salad bowl, run it through the dishwasher to be sure all the oil and residue are removed or the paint won't hold. Folk art painting is my favorite style. I use many birds with lots of fruit around them. On bowls like this I like to add checks around the top edge to give them an even more primitive look. I antiqued the piece with Umber oil paint mixed with a medium to get the soft, mellow look of age. I used the antiquing glaze to deepen the shadows and wipe out the highlight areas. When this was dry, I gave it a finishing coat of varnish.

Mary Jane Todd, CDA, *Red Bird in Fruit Bowl*, DecoArt Americana acrylic on salad bowl, 10″ (25cm) diameter × 5″ (13cm) deep

PRUDY VANNIER

Painting realistic fruit in acrylic is a challenge. The technique I used in *Pears* is a gradual layering of paint to make the subtle color changes and shading. I did the lettering using a flat brush and a basic calligraphy technique. The border incorporates carefully executed and spaced brushstrokes. Strokework and realistic painting complement each other when combined on one piece, but the two techniques must come together to create a successful design. In this case the color scheme unifies the design. With the pears' yellow color as the starting point, I added red to the rim of the plate and blue to the background to achieve a simple primary triadic color scheme.

Prudy Vannier, CDA, *Pears*, acrylic on wooden plate, 14″ (36cm) diameter

CHERI DENNETT, CDA

This bowl is part of a china set which had been in my husband's family for many years. I remember seeing it for the first time when he brought me home to meet his family and we walked in on a large dinner party! Now that the set is ours, we treasure it and our memories. I planned this painting carefully before I began. Due to the complexity of the china pattern, I wanted the painting to be simple, yet dramatic. I chose a gray-green for the background to complement the cherries and other pinks in the design. I hadn't intended to reproduce the reflection of the bowl, but when I set the bowl on a shiny surface, the reflection was wonderful! My biggest challenge in painting the reflection was to keep it almost attached to the bottom of the bowl, and yet keep it soft. I enjoyed solving these problems as I developed the painting.

Cheri Dennett, CDA, *Cherries in China*, oil on Masonite, 19½″ × 17½″ (50cm × 44cm)

MARY M. WISEMAN

When we recently spruced up our kitchen, I decided I wanted a brighter, more French country flare. The other pieces in my kitchen all have a fruit theme, so I designed this box to match, yet to incorporate the new, brighter color. I painted this design with Delta Ceramcoat and DecoArt Americana bottled acrylics, as they are the most available to the acrylic artist. Because both brands carry a wide range of hues, I was able to find all the colors I needed, eliminating the need for a lot of mixing.

Fruit is generally dark and heavy, but I wanted to create a look of softness and light. I gave the background a whitewashed look with a mixture of Dove Grey and White Lightning. I sponged in Driftwood to create a mottled background, then used more of this color to antique the lid, front and sides. To paint the fruit, I started with light, grayed-down values of color, building value changes slowly with lots of washes and glazing techniques. I enjoyed watching the colors come alive with each color glaze that I applied. Finally, I trimmed the box with Cape Cod Blue to pick up on the predominately blue color scheme in my kitchen.

Mary M. Wiseman, *Bread Box Fruit*, acrylic on wooden bread box, 6⅛″ × 16⅛″ (15.5cm × 40.9cm)

SUSIE SAUNDERS

The wonderful, primitive fruit designs of the talented folk artist Peter Ompir were the inspiration for this piece. The fine cupboard was made by a local cabinetmaker and was already stained. I used the traditional color scheme of dark red and black, sanding the black paint to allow the stain to show through in spots. I modified Ompir's technique of layering earth-tone glazes with the use of brighter and more vivid colors. I love color and had lots of fun adding tints of magenta, aqua, amethyst and

burgundy to my fruit. I based each piece of fruit with a "local" color and allowed it to dry. I then added many layers of transparent color to a retarder-moistened surface. I let each layer of glaze dry thoroughly before adding the next. One final bright sparkle gives life to the entire design. I did the antiquing on the cupboard door with retarder medium and burgundy plus black paint, then finished the piece with a hand-rubbed wax finish, which I love for fine furniture pieces.

Susie Saunders,
*Early American
Fruit Cupboard,*
acrylic gouache on
wooden cupboard,
17″ × 12″ × 6″
(43cm × 30cm × 15cm)

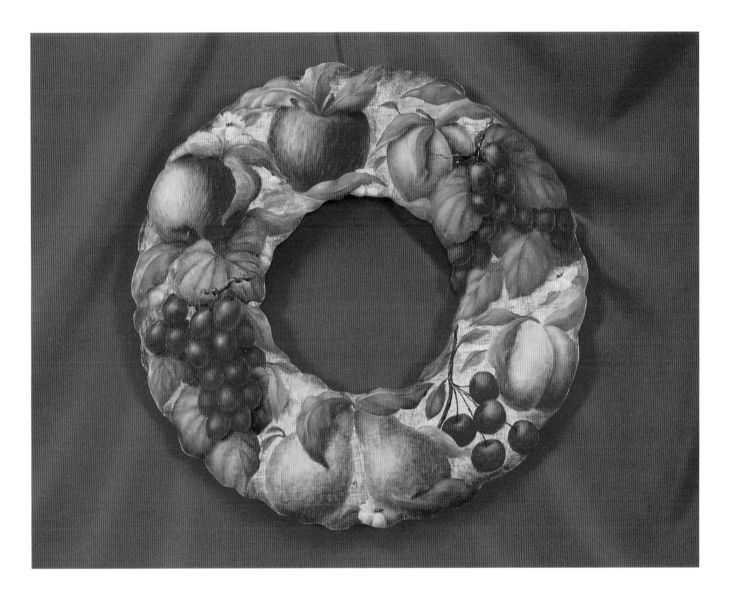

BETTY HERRON, CDA

When my woodcutting friend Howard called to say he'd finished cutting this pattern, he added, "That's the gosh darndest thing I ever cut." I couldn't wait to paint the wreath to show him why I wanted all those curves: I knew that each slight curve would give the final painting that extra special emphasis I wanted to achieve. I like the challenge of using different shapes of wood, glass or tin to help make my designs a little different than the ordinary. I knew I wanted a design with fruit, but not just a still life. A wreath of fruit was one way to accomplish an assorted fruit design. The wreath is cut from birch plywood. No sealer was used as I wanted the raw wood grain to show through the fruits to give them more texture.

As I painted each fruit, I had to keep the colors in harmony and try for a likeness, but also create varied textures to differentiate one fruit from another of the same kind. I chose reds to dominate throughout the design, making the apples the most detailed elements. These I based with medium and dark values, then pulled lights and highlights through where the light would

be strongest. The remaining fruit was simply pat blended with filbert brushes between light, medium and dark values. I used paint sparingly so the colors didn't become muddy. I added highlights and deep darks wet-on-wet. Rather than covering the entire wreath with fruit, I filled in around the fruits with leaves, keeping them simple so the fruit would be the primary interest. A few light blossoms helped lighten the painting.

When the paint was dry, I lightly touched accents and reflective colors onto the fruits and leaves, drybrushing where I wanted more texture and glazing where I wanted the area to remain smooth. When dry, I applied a wash of Burnt Umber in the negative spaces, causing the grain of the wood to look like a gauzy, fabric background. Finally, I slightly darkened the edges of the wreath with a sparse amount of straight Burnt Umber on a soft cloth.

Betty Herron, CDA, *Wreath of Fruit*, oil on wooden cutout, 10″ (25cm) diameter

VIRGINIA SMITH, CDA

I sealed this handmade bentwood box with Designs From the Heart wood sealer and based the background with two coats of Dark Forest Green acrylic. After spraying the surface with a light coat of Krylon Matte Spray, I traced my pattern onto the box. I often draw on tracing paper first so I can move the design elements around and see where I want to place them on the surface. I used a limited palette for this painting, mixing all the colors I needed from Cadmium Yellow, Yellow Ochre, Raw Sienna, Cadmium Red Light, Alizarin Crimson, Ultramarine Blue, Burnt Sienna, Burnt Umber, black and white. I started by laying in my lightest values, blending lightly between

colors as I painted. I like to brush mix as I paint, except when I paint leaves—I always mix several values of green before starting leaves. I paint each piece of fruit twice, the second time with a very thin glaze which adds additional color, dimension and softness. To finish the box, I antiqued the edges with black oil paint. When this was dry, I painted the little tole strokes with a small round brush, double-loaded with lighter values of the background color.

Virginia Smith, CDA, *Mixed Fruit*, oil over acrylic on bentwood box, 9″×7″×4″ (23cm×18cm×10.1cm)

JOAN M. WILDING, CDA

This design happened by what I call a "happy mistake." I originally ordered wooden plates to accompany a design by another artist. When I received the plates, I realized they were the wrong ones; the center of the plate was not large enough to accommodate the design. After calling the wholesaler and learning that there was a considerable restocking fee, I decided to keep the plates and come up with a new design. Having just completed a plate rack for my kitchen where I could display these plates, I decided fruit would be an appropriate theme. I had only designed and painted part of the fruit when my students began telling me they too wanted to paint this design. Some mistakes turn out with happy endings. Because most of my students are acrylic painters but I love the look of oils, I try to achieve the oil look by using many layers of acrylics, deepening each layer for shading and building my highlights gradually with successive layers. The center of the plate is faux finished and the bead is painted gold.

Joan M. Wilding, CDA, *Fruits A' Plenty*, acrylic on wooden plate, 14″ (36cm) diameter

LOUISE JACKSON, MDA

The challenge in painting this piece was that I wanted to create many apples and keep them all red. In doing so, I had to make some recede and some come forward without introducing new colors. I controlled this with contouring and highlights. There are easier ways to paint a barrel of apples—for instance, you could use yellow-green or orange in the focal apples so that the red apples would recede easily—but for this piece the red was as light as I wanted to go. Instead, I used less detail in the background apples and tried not to muddy them. I enjoy taking a simple subject and putting a new twist on it.

Louise Jackson, MDA, *Red Apples*, alkyd on wooden box, 18″ (46cm) diameter × 6″ (15cm) deep

PEGGY STOGDILL, MDA

This piece was inspired by pictures I'd seen of lush, "full-blown" arrangements, incorporating all sorts of fruits, vegetables and flowers. When I did the setup for the painting, I used an inexpensive basket I'd had around forever, because I was intrigued by the way the weave became smaller and changed direction at the bottom. The basket repeated the texture and feeling of the stained wood background I planned to use, but its pattern would keep it from being lost against the background. I included the nuts in the design for the same reason.

One of the objects in the arrangement is a partially ripe fig from the tree in our yard—people who've never seen a fresh fig sometimes think it's an onion! The wild grapevine is also from our backyard—I loved the interesting cast shadows it caused. I did the initial painting wet-on-wet. After the first stage was dry, I used multiple layers (drying between each layer) of transparent or semitransparent glazes, most often using a thin application of Winsor & Newton Blending and Glazing Medium on the object first to dampen the surface, enabling the blending of the pigment and ensuring transparency. In the glazing stage, values may be gradually built lighter or darker, details may be added or strengthened and color may be adjusted. For instance, in the first stage of this painting, the basket was too yellow, so when it was dry, I glazed it with a thin layer of Alizarin Crimson (using the glazing medium first). The sides of the box cover are very large so I wanted to keep them somewhat "quiet." I considered several options, but finally settled on a simple rag-rolled *faux* finish with some coordinating striping to break up the monotony.

Peggy Stogdill, MDA, *Bountiful*, oil on bentwood museum box, 8″ × 12″ × 17″ (20cm × 30cm × 43cm)

Brenda McPeek, CDA, *Graniteware and Blueberries*, oil over acrylic on Masonite panel, 22″×19″×4″ (56cm×48cm×10cm)

3
REALISTIC STILL LIFE

The human eye seeks beauty everywhere. This beauty can be found almost anywhere, but there is no better place than right at home. Even a random arrangement of household items can be a delight to the eye and to the mind. Forms, shapes, colors and shadows make memorable images that the artist can preserve in paint, capturing the everyday pleasures others often overlook.

Memories associated with hearth and home can be evoked by the simplest things—a mixing bowl like Mom's, a tablecloth, a childhood toy. A still life, a collection randomly or artfully arranged, can offer a medley of memories. A still life may be made up of stationary objects, motionless and tranquil, but it is truly representative of the essence of human life.

BRENDA McPEEK, CDA

I dreamed this project up as a girlfriend and I were "antiquing." I collect graniteware and enamelware, and enjoy the pieces both as painting surfaces and as subject matter. After purchasing the blue swirl teapot and "eye-spying" a garland of blueberries, the planning process began, right in the antique store! I based this project in acrylics and embellished it in oils. This method produces a very developed, finished look, making painters of all levels feel very accomplished. It is also a gentle way to introduce oils to a new (or old) painter.

Brenda McPeek, CDA, *Graniteware and Blueberries*, oil over acrylic on Masonite panel, 22″ × 19″ × 4″ (56cm × 48cm × 10cm)

JANET G. SNELL

The inspiration for this design and its colors comes from my love of collecting antique kitchenware pieces and Americana. I picked the recipe box for this design because I like to paint my designs on useful items. Since today's kitchens are lighter and brighter in look and feel, I chose to stain the nondesign area of this box with DecoArt Americana Bleached White Pine acrylic gel stain. I worked from a photo of the actual setup, using a right-hand light source. When painting in acrylics, I like to use the Suzie's Pit-I-Pat brush to soften my floats. Using this techique it is sometimes necessary to do the floats twice, but I feel that it gives a more realistic look. I also do a lot of color mixing with DecoArt Americana bottle acrylics to get the color I want. I did the finishing trim with the blue mix from the cup as line work and then spattered on the white. Finally I protected the piece with Blair Satin Tole spray varnish.

Janet G. Snell,
Red, White and Blue Recipe Box, acrylic on wooden recipe box, 7½″ × 7″ × 9″ (19cm × 18cm × 23cm)

CAROL-LEE CISCO, CDA

I originally designed this piece to hold my credit card imprinter on the tabletop of my booth at conventions and shows. When I'm not at shows, it serves as a place to put files of pieces in progress so they are handy and all in one place; hence the title *Getting Organized*. The design shows the various stages of creating a piece from beginning to end, including the paint mixtures and formula used in painting this piece. I used the *trompe l'oeil* technique to paint this piece: The objects are life-size, have the proper perspective, contain shadows and appear to "invade" the viewer's space—such as the open drawer and pencil hanging over the edge of the shelf. The shadows were particularly fun to do. They're painted with transparent paint

and really give dimension and realism to flat objects. I painted the clear tape holding the paint chips with one stroke of transparent white; so simple, yet so effective. This piece can be personalized with favorite book titles, familiar names and phone numbers. In the notes and lists on the right side, I included the names of the first class I taught when my studio opened, the deadlines for submitting to teach at shows, etc. This is an easy design to paint and can be easily converted to acrylics.

Carol-Lee Cisco, CDA, *Getting Organized*, oil on wooden file box, 6½" × 11½" × 17" (17cm × 29cm × 43cm)

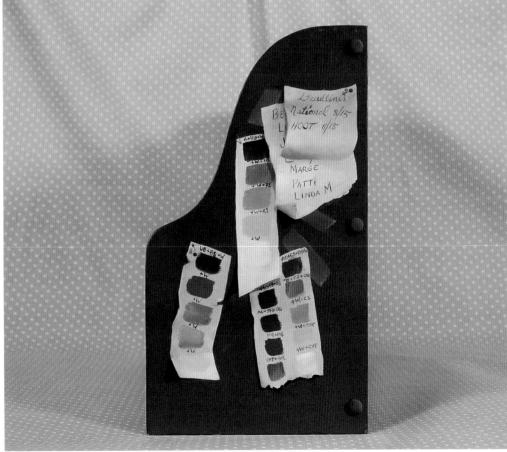

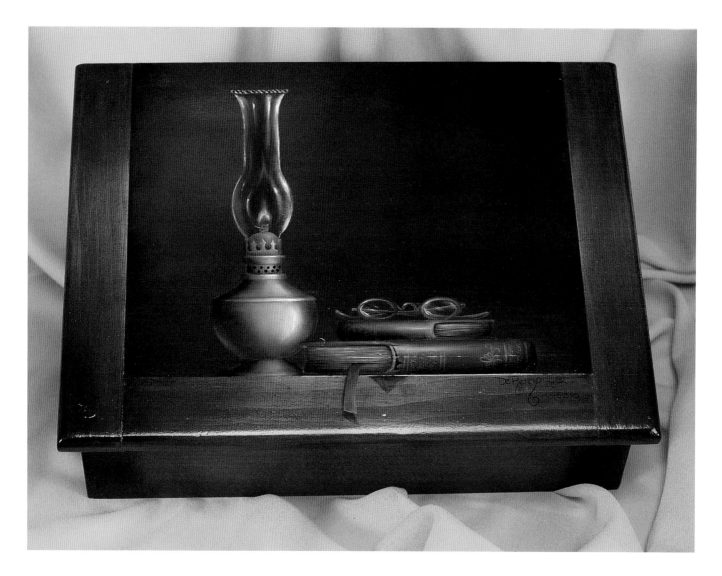

PATTI J. DeRENZO, CDA

This still life, painted in Jo Sonja Chroma acrylics, is an example of *trompe l'oeil* (French for "to fool the eye"). The design makes it appear that the Bible and the ribbon bookmark hang over the front edge of the shelf. The challenge of this piece was to use an eye-level perspective and convince the eye, through the control of value, that there is depth within the composition. This piece forced me to re-create the textures of three very different types of surfaces: glass, metal and leather. I found the reflective characteristics of each substance particularly challenging. I chose an upper, right-hand light source and used overall dark values to help intensify the minimal uses of lights and highlights. I did this piece with my blended acrylic method. Every piece I paint has an accompanying scripture. This piece was inspired by the Bible verse, "Thy word is a lamp unto my feet, and a light unto my path" (Psalms 119:105). Of course such divine inspiration could only be painted on a slant-top Bible box!

Patti J. DeRenzo, CDA, *Thy Word Is a Lamp Unto My Feet*, acrylic on Bible box, 6″ × 14″ × 9¾″ (15cm × 36cm × 25cm)

TINA SUE NORRIS

Collecting leaves was my very favorite part of grade school science classes, and I'm still collecting. Since collecting anything can get out of hand, I usually collect the leaves, photograph their beautiful shapes and colors in various arrangements, then "set them free." There are, however, those few leaves that just beg to be waxed and saved for future reference and admiration. I thought it would be nice to have a place to keep an assortment of nature's jewels handy for quick reference when painting or drawing. I soon found the box was a wonderful conversation piece for a coffee table; visitors are always intrigued when they open the box to find the waiting captives.

When creating this piece, I wanted the background to give a feeling of the forest floor. I used a base of antique gold and sponged on some leaf colors of red and green, then used a black faux finish over all, lifting and texturing the wet black with crumpled plastic wrap. I based the leaves, cones and berries with acrylics, using a medium value of the color desired for each element. I added the shading and highlighting with a glazing technique, which can be done with alkyds or oils. I especially enjoy glazing with alkyds as they dry quickly and the painting can be added to as often as desired. In fact, many times I will leave the piece unvarnished and return years later to add more details or color. I usually use a light coat of Krylon Matte 1311 for protection after each subsequent application of paint.

Tina Sue Norris, *Leaf Collector's Box*, acrylic and alkyd on round bentwood box, 13″ (33cm) diameter

JUDY DIEPHOUSE

When I saw this piece with its large painting surface, I knew it would be perfect for a still-life design. Spices and herbs make me think of Italian cooking, so I felt the makings of an Italian dinner would be an appropriate subject for this spice cabinet. Since the insert is reversible, I also designed a holiday still life on the other side so the piece can be used all year long. To paint the crocks, I rewet the basecoated crock with clean water, applied the shade color in the proper area and softly mopped it with a mop brush to achieve a soft shading. I used the same method to add the highlights. To paint the bottles, I washed over the entire glass area with a thin wash of the bottle color, then reinforced the edges of the bottle with a side-loaded float of the bottle color mixed with a touch of white. I added some thin streaks of white to create the shine lines. Adding details along the shelf—such as the vines or ribbons with leaves—helps connect all the objects in the still life.

Judy Diephouse, *Italian Dinner Spice Cabinet With Holiday Insert*, acrylic on wooden spice cabinet, 18″ × 15″ × 4½″ (46cm × 38cm × 11.4cm)

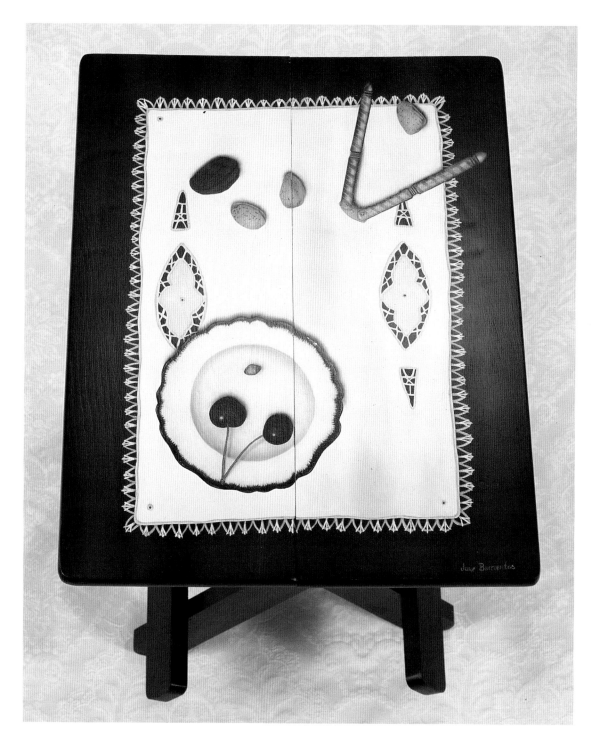

JANE BARRIENTOS, CDA

Currently, *trompe l'oeil* designs are my favorite to paint. It's easy for viewers to get involved with the designs—some need to touch the surface to assure themselves the objects are really only painted. Most of my work is done in oil. I like the texture, the actual painting time is shorter and by using a medium of linseed oil and Damar varnish, it is dry by the next day. The folding table is practical for storage and useful in small spaces. Since many of my students are looking for tabletop designs, I combined objects that would be associated with a casual snack and rearranged them until I liked the pattern they made. I tried to keep the design colors quiet, so this piece could be used in most homes for a long period of time. I sanded and sealed the piece and painted the design in oil. Most of the furniture in my home is cherry or mahogany, so I painted the table with a mixture of Raw Sienna, Alizarin Crimson and Burnt Umber to match the stain on my other pieces. My students each stained their tables to match their own furniture. I finished the table with five coats of varnish.

Jane Barrientos, CDA, *Cherries and Nuts,* oil on wooden table, 14″ × 18″ × 30″ (36cm × 46cm × 76cm)

LESLIE SMITH, CDA

I'm always on the prowl for old pieces with character; this table was found at a local thrift shop. Designs are my way of telling a story or conveying a feeling. Often, I encourage others to reminisce about someone they remember fondly, a favorite childhood memory or a subject about which they feel passionately. As they speak, I close my eyes and before long I see the next design take form. I then go to my stockpile of "found" treasures and pick a surface to match the time period and style of the design. This table was easy. A friend was talking about her grandmother, Violet. Violet had lots of old lace and liked to sew. My friend loved to play with all the pretty things in

her grandmother's attic. I have repeated this design on an old chest and a sewing box, against different backgrounds. I created this faux finish background with sponged acrylic paint, softened with a huge mop brush and accented with oils. I executed the *trompe l'oeil* elements (French for "to fool the eye") in oils and alkyds. I usually protect heavy wear areas, like this tabletop, with as many as fifteen coats of brush-on varnish.

Leslie Smith, CDA, *Just an Old Fashioned Nosegay*, oil over acrylic on wooden tabletop, 16″ (41cm) diameter

A. JOAN LOCKYEAR, CDA

I love to arrange my "stuff" in still-life compositions to tell a story. The inspiration for this piece started with the tin of maple syrup and the box of "sold only in Canada" Red Rose Tea. The flour bag, bowl, spoon and blueberries are to suggest blueberry pancakes, thus the title, *Canadian Breakfast*. The actual colors of the flour, tea bag and maple syrup containers suggested an analogous color scheme using yellow, orange and red. The touches of blue and turquoise add accents from the opposite side of the color wheel. I develop my designs by photographing the still-life setup with my 35mm camera, using a 60 watt lamp on an adjustable stand as the light source, rather than a flash, and 400 ASA film. This gives me a good representation of the light and shadow in the design. I then enlarge the photograph to the desired size on a black-and-white photocopier, giving me a ready-to-trace design. Photo-graphing a still-life setup in this way ensures an accurate drawing and correct perspective. I painted this design with a pat-blended, dry-brush technique using short chisel blenders to establish the underpainting. I applied the stripes, lettering, cracks in the bowl and other details with transparent layers of paint glazed over the dried underpainting. I achieved the warm glow on the wood cabinet with a mixture of Raw Sienna and Burnt Umber oils, thinned down with Archival Classic Me-dium, then applied as a stain. I further antiqued the edges with straight Burnt Umber. When the piece was completely dry, I protected it with three coats of varnish.

A. Joan Lockyear, CDA, *Canadian Breakfast,* oil on Masonite panel in wooden cabinet, 15½″ × 4″ × 13″ (39cm × 10.1cm × 33cm)

SANDRA S. CODDAIRE, CDA

While at a local antique market, I came upon the small, unusual piece of enamelware featured in this design. It immediately brought to mind images of schoolchildren skipping down country lanes, books and lunches in hand, on the way to an old-fashioned one-room country school. For my design, I settled on an eye-level still life, incorporating the "pitcher," my father's old schoolbooks, a toy top and, of course, an apple for the teacher, all rendered on a background of black, reminiscent of old chalkboards. After searching for just the right piece, I decided on the miniature lap desk to continue the school theme. I painted the design in oils with a limited palette of primary colors (red, yellow and blue) for simplicity. Undercoating the container was necessary to facilitate painting it on such a dark background. I employed glazing techniques to add shadows and dimension. Because I was striving to invoke a nostalgia for days long since past, the remainder of the desk was stained to keep the piece simple. Finally, I treated the entire piece to several coats of varnish to make it usable.

Sandra S. Coddaire, CDA, *Hoosier School Days,* oil on miniature lap desk, 8″ × 9″ × 3″ (20cm × 23cm × 7.6cm)

Dorothy Dent, *Summer Evening*, oil on wooden box, 7″ × 11″ × 15½″ (18cm × 28cm × 39cm)

4

HEARTWARMING SCENES

*M*emories make for a rich store of subject material for the artist. Decorative painting has as part of its charm certain implicit values such as a celebration of family, of friends, a love for the land, the simpler joys of life. A painted scene evocative of these values lets us hold these things for savoring, for inspiration and contemplation.

The following artworks—through a tranquil view, a memory of childhood haunts, of a light glowing in a window—invite us to slip peacefully into a revery of those times in our own lives when happiness came unannounced.

DOROTHY DENT

In 1996 I was fortunate enough to go to England for two weeks. I so enjoyed seeing and photographing the old stone buildings, thatched-roof cottages and beautiful countryside that make England the wonderful and historic country it is. Back at home, I began painting from my photographic "treasure trove." Photos can be used for inspiration and reference, but I never hesitate to use my artistic license to move things around for a better composition, adding this or taking out that, until the sketch pleases me. I then transfer the line drawing to the object to be painted. This particular scene is from Burton-on-the-Water, a quaint village of ancient stone buildings with a lovely stream meandering through it all. Although it was daytime when I took the photo, I decided to make the painting a late evening scene so I could have the lights shining from the windows, creating a feeling of warmth and comfort which helps to draw the viewer into the painting. This piece could be done in oils or acrylics. I work in both mediums, but my first love is oil—its richness and depth of color is more intense than other mediums. When working with oils, I allow for more drying time before layering color on top of color. I speed this process up by using Winsor & Newton white alkyd along with my regular oils. The use of a paint medium that contains a dryer, such as Winsor & Newton's Liquin, also makes the paint tack up a bit faster.

Dorothy Dent, *Summer Evening*, oil on wooden box, 7" × 11" × 15½" (18cm × 28cm × 39cm)

BILL DeLOACH

At one of our yearly family gatherings not long after Grandma passed away, several family members were reminiscing about her and how much she loved to knit. When the old photo album containing a picture of her house was passed around, I decided to paint this piece for my mother. She and Grandma were very close, and when I presented the box to her on Grandma's birthday, she tearfully told me I could not have given her a more special gift. I prepared the box with a coat of denatured alcohol and clear shellac mixed half and half. I gave the entire surface a light sanding, then masked off the area to be painted and primed it with a coat of gesso to provide a suitable painting surface. I captured the old homestead and water cistern as they existed; however, I took artistic license with the location of the outhouse and river. For the sake of the composition, I also removed all but one of the live oaks that surrounded the house. Granny's wild iris blooms at the base of the tree and the summer sky bring the scene to life once more. I left the rest of the box its natural color and finished the entire piece with two coats of shellac.

Bill DeLoach, *Grandma's Knitting Box*, archival artist oil on oval bentwood box, 10″ × 6½″ × 16″ (25cm × 17cm × 41cm)

DIANE BEGINNES-PHALEN

I wanted *Summer Memories* to be a culmination of everything that makes the summer special, from the lazy days spent on a porch swing enjoying a book, nap or glass of lemonade, to the trips to the seashore complete with lighthouse, kites, sailboats and seagulls enjoying the summer breeze. I started this painting with the ocean background. I blended the sky, water and background trees using various wet-on-wet washes of Cerulean Blue and Cobalt Blue for the sky and Sap Green and Permanent Green for the distant firs. The background elements are all rendered with soft washes so they don't compete with the foreground. The Adirondack chairs and beach umbrella are rendered with sharp, crisp lines and washes to focus the middle of the painting. I angled the porch to point to the lighthouse and horizon, allowing the viewer's eye to move easily through the painting. The porch must show depth, so once again I rendered the back areas with soft washes and less detail. I used several layers of wet-on-wet washes of Cobalt

Blue and Cerulean Blue in the shadows under the eaves and porch. I rendered the middle flowers loosely with wet washes and less detail than the foreground flowers, then further toned them down with a wash of Cobalt Blue to allow them to blend behind the brighter foreground flowers, creating depth. I first glazed the reds of the roses and trumpeter vine flowers with Fluorescent Red gouache to give the flowers an additional glow of color, then applied several glazes of Cadmium Red, allowing each layer to dry before applying additional color. I used Alizarin Crimson in the deeper shadows of the petals. Finally, I finished the background kites and seagulls using colors from elsewhere in the painting. *Summer Memories* will bring warm thoughts through even the coldest winter months.

Diane Beginnes-Phalen, *Summer Memories*, transparent watercolor and gouache on 555 lb. D'Arches cold-pressed watercolor paper, 29″ × 41″ (74cm × 104cm)

SHARON BUONONATO, CDA

I live in the Hudson River Valley, so it was only natural to include the Catskill Mountains and Hudson River in this autumn scene. Living in a historic village—Rhinebeck, New York was founded in 1688 and boasts ties to a long list of famous people and events throughout New York's history—I wanted to express some of the history of my area, combined with today's decorative painting techniques and functional surfaces. I chose to paint this landscape in a style reminiscent of the masters of the Hudson River School of Art, a group of talented artists painting at the turn of the century who went out into nature along the river valley and mountains to sketch and paint the beautiful views. I basecoated the box with sky

blue, then completed the scene and the floral borders. The lady with her parasol and faithful dog were added to capture the romance of the turn of the century. I then basecoated the rims of the box in two warm tones and decorated them with copper strokework. The copper detailing is repeated in the mums, leaves, vines and berries, creating a warm, autumn color scheme. To finish the aged appearance, the entire box was glazed with transparent oils in a rich, dark brown.

Sharon Buononato, CDA, *Catskill Autumn*, gouache and oil glazing on wooden Bombay box, 12″ × 8½″ × 5″ (30cm × 22cm × 13cm)

RUTH DOLSEN

This basket would make the perfect holder for more items than I can list here (needlework, plants, napkins, dried flowers, potpourri, letters/bills) and it will fit into the informal home as well as the traditional setting. Almost everyone likes rural houses and other scenes of Americana because they are so warm and inviting. After basecoating the sides with the sky color, block in the buildings and landscape. Then add the bricks, windows and other details. I smudged the clouds in with my finger to provide a nice contrast to the straight lines of the design. After the painting has dried overnight, add all

the shading with oil antiquing—one step does it all. The trim can be done in any color used in the design. Protect the surface with waterbased varnish; the number of coats depends on how you intend to use the basket. The inside can be stained, painted or lined with fabric. Adapt this design to fit a recipe box, pencil holder or a great flea market find to create a complementary piece for your basket—one piece is never enough!

Ruth Dolsen, *Americana Basket*, acrylic on bentwood basket with oil antiquing, 6½″ × 8″ × 10″ (17cm × 20cm × 25cm)

CATHERINE HOLMAN

I loved the idea of this box which has four separate compartments to divide assorted flavors of tea bags. It reminded me of an antique pencil box. I painted this box with various shades of teal green and rusty red, which are colors used in today's interior decorating. Since this box is meant to hold tea bags, I decided to add a cozy little Tea Shoppe when I designed this quaint fishing village. You could add your own touches by personalizing the names on some of the buildings. To give the grass some texture, I stippled in the distant land area with an old, fuzzy flat brush using light shades of green plus touches of pale yellow. I did all the shading and highlighting by dampening the area first, applying the float with a side-loaded flat brush and quickly but gently mopping over the area with a large mop brush to soften it. I protected the finish with two to three coats of a waterbased matte varnish.

Catherine Holman, *Village of Stoney Point*, acrylic on tea bag box, 14″ × 5½″ × 3″ (36cm × 14cm × 7.6cm)

SHARON ARCHER, CDA

On a very warm July day several years ago, I went to my studio to paint for some enjoyment (which doesn't happen too often). This sled had been previously sealed, sanded and basecoated in a dark forest green. I picked it up and began to sketch the buildings with a white chalk pencil—the design just seemed to fall off the pencil. It didn't take long for me to decide on a winter scene. Growing up on a farm in Ohio gave me great material for the design. After the landscape was painted, the sled still looked as if it was missing something. That's when I decided to add the branches, leaves and berries. Since I wanted the viewer to notice and enjoy the scene first, I painted the berries and leaves with less detail. The painting brings back many happy childhood memories of sledding with my brothers. I hope it sparks some favorite winter memory of yours.

Sharon Archer, CDA,
Country Winter Sled,
oil over acrylic on
wooden sled, 15½″ × 9″
(39cm × 23cm)

LOIS GIVEN

While on one of our trips to Ireland, my husband, Bob, and I came upon this "welcoming committee" on the road leading from Galway Bay to the Cliffs of Mohr. The cows looked as though they were expecting us, and made no attempt to move when my husband stopped the car and stepped out to take a photograph. When we came home and went through our pictures, I immediately knew I had to put this scene on canvas. I worked directly from the photograph with two minor changes: I changed the blacktop road in the photograph to a dirt road to create a warmer, "Old Country" feel, and I took artistic license by turning a white cow into a black one. To capture the greens of the "Emerald Isle," I used seven shades of green oil paint, including Chromium Oxide and Olive Greens with limited amounts of Cadmium Yellow and white. I normally use filbert brushes to paint the foliage in my *Highlands and Hedgerows* books, but to capture the lush trees and vegetation in this scene, I found that my oldest, most "scrubby" brushes worked best, with the help of some rounds and filberts to achieve the "dibby-dab" technique. The haze in the background was done after the foliage was throughly dry. I spattered the road to give a gravel effect, and finished the painting with satin acrylic spray.

Lois Given,
Welcoming Committee,
oil on canvas,
16″ × 18″
(41cm × 46cm)

Sherry C. Nelson, MDA, *A Touch of Gold—Yellow Warbler*, oil and gold leaf on turned basswood plate, 18″ (46cm) diameter

5

COLORFUL WILDLIFE

*I*t is no surprise that some of man's first works of art, dancing across the dark cave walls in tones of sepia and burnt umber, depicted animals. Humankind reveres our wild brethren for their unique beauty and character—the bright colors of plumage, the soft textures of fur—and for the very freedom that makes them different from us.

But we also see in animals reflections of ourselves. Many artists strive to capture the lonely sadness of the wolf, the sleepy contentment of a cat, the comic arrogance of the peacock.

Animals are a challenging enterprise for the painter. The subjects are never still. Their forms are as complicated as they are fascinating. Their texture, fur, feathers, paws and claws all demand close observation and understanding by the artist to render them convincingly in paint. This chapter shows how decorative painters rise to the challenge to capture the grace and strength of the animals around us.

SHERRY C. NELSON, MDA

This unusual basswood plate was turned by Paul Loftness of Gibbon, Minnesota. As I began the designing process for the plate, it seemed it would be an interesting tie-in to paint a graceful branch of basswood leaves and buds. To make the rich, dark greens of the leaves meld softly with the background, I chose a black acrylic basecoat, antiqued with softened splotches of greens. This made the perfect setting for the tiny warbler, whose plumage shone brightly against the greens, creating the focal area of the design. Yellow warblers are found commonly across most of North America in the summer months. The little male, with his distinctive rusty streaking, is shown in this painting, making it a subject that would be appreciated by most bird enthusiasts. The final "touch of gold"

was added with the wide gold-leafed border. I used Red Oxide acrylic under the gold leaf to warm the tones, and antiqued the leafed area with a bit of Burnt Umber oil paint to further heighten the interest. The use of gold leaf gives a more formal look to the piece; if your home is more rustic, this area could be stained or painted in an alternate color. After the background detailing and the painting was complete, I used a spray satin varnish (oil-base, since the piece is painted in oils) for my final finish.

Sherry C. Nelson, MDA, *A Touch of Gold—Yellow Warbler*, oil and gold leaf on turned basswood plate, 18″ (46cm) diameter

KARL-HEINZ MESCHBACH, CGCDP

Early samples of reverse painting on glass have survived in Roman glass of the third and fourth century AD. Modern glass painting, called *Verre Eglomise*, is named after Jean Baptiste Glomi, who is said to have revived the early technique in about 1760. My painting is inspired by the glass painting style of the late-nineteenth- and early-twentieth-century sign painters of the Western and Central European Painters Guild. Many of these works were executed in commercial environments: butcher shops and other retail stores, restaurants, and most notably on pub signs and windows. This technique also found use in jewelry, furniture and other functional as well as decorative elements. A mirror would tradi-

tionally first be painted, then "silvered." Since today's technology affords us a better-quality mirror silvering, I was intrigued to try another route. After working out the design, I had the mirror cut and beveled. I then gently sandblasted the negative design out of the silver. From there on I executed the work in the usual manner for reverse painting, which is an entire reversal of the normal painting process: the first stroke made is actually the one that will show up on top of the finished design and vice versa. Any blending of color has to be deep and complete, and each stroke has to be precisely placed.

Karl-Heinz Meschbach, CGCDP, *Birds of a Feather*, oil behind glass mirror, 20″ × 36″ (51cm × 91cm)

JOHN GUTCHER

Much of my painting is done in the style of the Old Masters, who preferred to paint on wood because its durability allowed them to paint with extreme detail. Designing this graceful peacock in a lush garden setting gave me the opportunity to create a scene of soft, elegant beauty, highlighted by a natural, off-white background. I sealed and primed the raw wood with J.W. Etc. White Lightning, giving it a soft, whitewashed appearance which enhances the wood grain. I use Permalba oils for their pure, clean colors, quality and creamy consistency. A combination of the proper consistency of paint, medium and a fine liner brush give me many hours of pleasure when painting detailed feathers and/or hair. To achieve a high level of realism when painting the peacock's tail, I tied individual feathers together into a mock "tail" and positioned them with the proper lighting, painting them as I would a still-life setup.

It was only natural to have one *trompe l'oeil* feather positioned on top of the box. This single feather became an extremely interesting and challenging in-depth study in itself. The fine details and iridescent colors in the bulb of the feather are very attractive. I created the iridescent blues and greens with Phthalo Blue and Phthalo Green mixtures; when lightened with Titanium White, they take on a glowing brilliance. Using many layers of overlapping strokes, I built up the texture and tonal value of the fine hairs of the feather, working from dark to light. The curve of the feather is accentuated with soft, gray shadows underneath, creating the *trompe l'oeil* effect. People have actually tried to pick the feather up!

John Gutcher, *Peacock and Trompe L'Oeil Feather*, oil on oval wooden "bride's box," 20″ × 12″ × 8½″ (51cm × 30cm × 22cm)

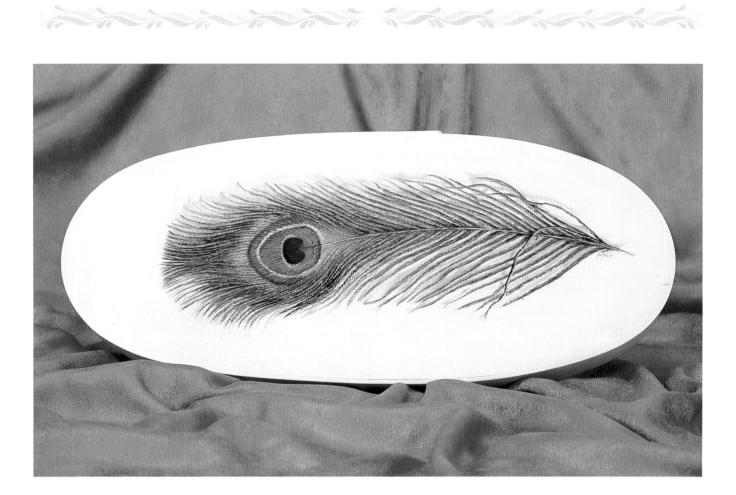

SHARON STANSIFER, CDA

There were several challenges in creating this design. I wanted the eyes of the alert baby bobcat to portray his charm and innocence as he snuggles safely with his contented sleeping brother (I decided they were both boys because I have two sons). To capture the transparent appearance of the eyes and create their sparkle is critical; in this way, painting eyes is very similar to painting waterdrops. To create the realistic fur, I pulled the fur strokes in several colors back and forth into each other—a technique called color weaving. It takes a little patience, but the reward is well worthwhile. I used a special brush that enables me to build a wonderful, deep texture to the fur. I used a crackling technique to create the bark texture of the fallen log on which the bobcats are resting. The wood piece with the naturally barked edges I selected for these beautiful babies seemed a perfect choice—it gives the woodsy finish I was looking for.

Sharon Stansifer, CDA, *Sleepy Baby Bobcats*, acrylic on natural bark basswood plank, 13″ × 10½″ (33cm × 27cm)

DOROTHY WHISENHUNT, CDA

I think the "country look" is here to stay. This particular project is one of three nesting chipwood boxes. The largest box is painted with a crowing rooster and the smallest box with baby chicks. A good friend, Greg, came up with the neat idea to have a wooden egg nestled into Spanish moss in the smallest box. I've painted this series in oils and acrylics. For both mediums, I begin by painting the background with a light ivory acrylic. If painting in oils, I then mist the boxes with Krylon Matte 1311, then use a wet-on-wet technique. If painting in acrylics, I paint in thin layers. After the design is dry, I spray it with Krylon Satin Varnish spray 7002 to protect the painting and give the boxes a soft sheen.

Dorothy Whisenhunt, CDA, *Nestin' Instinct*, oil over acrylic on chipwood box, 4″ × 3″ × 2″ (10.1cm × 7.6cm × 5cm)

LuANNE MURPHY

The painting surface for *Spirit Wolf* began its life as a buckeye root. I had just gotten home from a photo shoot of timber wolves in Minnesota when I received this box. There was no question what had to be painted on it. By incorporating the wolves with the wood grain, burls, cracks, crevices and knotholes, a free-form effect is achieved. I chose the only space large enough on the front of the box to accommodate the entire wolf face. The placement of knotholes determined which way the head needed to be facing. The box arrived sanded and sealed, so I simply traced the drawing onto the wooden surface with white graphite paper. I painted the wolf wet-on-wet, using a painting medium for easier blending and faster drying. I left some midtone areas of the hair unpainted, letting the natural wood tones show through. I used white, black and Burnt Umber for the lightest hair and Yellow Ochre, Raw Sienna and Burnt Sienna for the yellow and brown tones. For the eyes I used a bit of Terra Rosa along with the yellow and brown tones. To paint the hair I used a liner to sketch the hair in, deepened the dark shadows with a small sable flat, used a rake brush to pull up light gray hairs, then added a few detailed hairs in a lighter gray with a small liner. I used the rake brush alone for the sketchy outer hair and let the natural wood grain show through.

This is the perfect piece for wispy, furtive figures, slipping away into a natural crevice or wood canyon. By letting the wood piece suggest placement of the oil sketches, each creation is a "one of a kind" and as unique as the tree it came from.

LuAnne Murphy, *Spirit Wolf*, oils on nested burl wood box, 10″×8″×3″ (25cm×20cm×7.6cm)

DOROTHY EGAN

This piece was designed to fit on an antique slant-top desk in our dining room. There is a flat area at the back of the desk before it begins to slant that is perfectly suited to hold a piece like this. Because the desk is an antique, I wanted the wood piece to have the same time-worn look. First I used a wood rasp and coarse sandpaper to round off all edges and corners, simulating the wear that occurs after long use. Next I applied wood sealer to the entire piece and painted the front of the box with a mushroom-colored acrylic, leaving a ¼-inch border of raw wood to "frame" the design. I painted the goose and

goslings with oil, using Liquin as a medium. When the painting was dry, I stained all the exposed wood with Raw Umber plus Burnt Umber oils, thinned with odorless paint thinner. I used the same mixture to antique the edges of the painted surface. When thoroughly dry, I applied several coats of good quality polyurethane satin varnish.

Dorothy Egan, *Canada Goose Desk Caddy*, oil on wooden letter and pencil holder, 4″ × 12″ × 4″ (10cm × 30cm × 10cm)

LIN WELLFORD

Rocks are a great resource for painters. What other surface offers the chance to mimic reality so convincingly, and so inexpensively? On top of that, searching out just the right rock is a big part of the fun. Use rocks that are smooth with rounded contours. Nature photographs can help you match rock shapes to particular animal subjects. The possibilities are endless: fawns, foxes, raccoons, penguins and owls, even frogs and bugs. I basecoated this tiger with Burnt Sienna craft acrylic (you can use artist quality acrylics or even oil if you prefer). When dry, I sketched on the design with white chalk. To create shadows and emphasize shapes, I added black to the Burnt Sienna to create a deep brown. To create highlights, I blended Yellow Ochre along the top of the head, haunch and

tail. I then used a medium-sized brush to add black stripes and white markings, using a photograph for placement. To paint the fine features such as the fur and eye outlines, a long script liner brush in a size 0 or 1 works best. Try to vary the fur lines, changing the angles of individual strokes and altering the paint shades to add visual interest. Keep in mind that most animal fur grows back from the nose toward the tail. The more fur you paint, the more realistic and appealing your finished piece will be. A coat of clear polyurethane will enrich the colors and protect the surface.

Lin Wellford, *Tiger Rock*, acrylic on rock, 6½″ × 8½″ × 5″ (17cm × 22cm × 13cm)

MARY McCULLAH, CDA

This painting was inspired by the beauty and strength of a captive-born wolf pack at Bays Mountain Nature Preserve in Kingsport, Tennessee. As a volunteer, I helped socialize Askina—whose name in the Cherokee language means ghost or spirit—from the time she was six weeks old until she joined our adults at about four months old.

I prepared the background with a sponge roller and alternating values of gray and off-white. The sponge roller gives a nice tooth to the surface, which is then lightly sanded. Acrylic gouache, when used as a retarder, allows for an extended open time for painting wet-into-wet. This technique achieves a soft, natural look. I work with a dirty brush as often as possible, brush mixing colors. The color scheme is basically warm, with the use of Payne's Gray to create cool accents. I painted Askina

with earth tones of grays, Raw Sienna, Brown Earth, Burnt Umber, Payne's Gray and black.

When working with fur, I follow three basic steps: a foundation of paint to establish value and color, detailing in layers to create realism and further shade and highlight and final glazing to adjust value and tone. When painting fur, consider its growth direction and value change. Adjust the brushstroke to match the length of the fur. The eyes deserve equal attention to detail—this is the area that attracts the viewer, creates emotion and brings the creature to life.

Mary McCullah, CDA, *Berry Patch Beauty—Askina*, acrylic gouache on gessoed Masonite panel, 16″ × 20″ (41cm × 51cm)

DeLANE LANGE

I decided to paint this piece as a wedding chest for my youngest daughter, Gini. She loves pastels and birds, so I knew where to begin. I had received a small camelback trunk from Valhalla Designs in Glendale, Oregon, and had decided this would be a lovely trunk to paint especially for Gini's big day. I thought the lovebirds in pastel colors would be both beautiful and romantic—lovebirds have been a symbol of love and romance for many years, so they were a natural choice in creating a functional gift with a meaningful design. I chose to do decorative line work on the ends of the trunk—the cross-hatching in soft greens creates a pleasing border against the Antique White of the center. Marbleizing with the same colors would also be very effective. The birds are shaded and then glazed with soft colors from the flowers and leaves. The flowers and leaves are generally floated and lightened from the outside

edge toward the center with the chisel edge of the brush. The rows of golden scrolls add color and interest to the edges of the design.

The wedding was so lovely, and it meant so much to me to be able to share this special day and heirloom with my daughter and her husband. On a long table, opposite the cake with its pearls and roses, the chest was opened just a little, in front of a champagne fountain. Flowers spilled onto the lace tablecloth. It was absolutely beautiful. A special day for a very special couple. I hope you will enjoy this piece, and have the opportunity to paint an anniversary trunk to enhance another special couple's big day.

DeLane Lange, *Anniversary Trunk*, acrylic on wooden trunk, 13″ × 16″ × 10½″ (33cm × 41cm × 27cm)

CLAUDIA NICE

This rabbit painting was inspired by the generations of cotton-tails that have lived under our blackberry thicket, kept safe from coyotes and hawks by the thorny tangle. Quite often I would see the rabbits peeking out from their leafy dens, surrounded by the ripening fruit of late summer. The rabbit study began as a pen-and-ink drawing on watercolor paper. I used a .25 Rapidograph pen, filled with Universal Black India ink (Koh-I-Noor 3080). This particular ink is very brushproof, allowing me to overlay the pen work with washes of watercolor. I used washes of Burnt Sienna mixed with Burnt Umber to bring the crisscross strokes of rabbit fur to life. I tinted the ripe berries with Alizarin Crimson, a mixture of Burnt Sienna

and Payne's Gray and Ultramarine Blue, making them appear good enough to eat. (In fact, that's just what I did with the berries I was using as a reference for this painting!) The leaves were simply outlincd and tinted with a mix of Permanent Green Light and Burnt Sienna so they wouldn't compete with the more involved parts of the painting. To adapt this design to a wooden surface, ink it over a light acrylic background and tint it with thin washes of oil paint.

Claudia Nice, *Rabbit in the Blackberry Brambles*, pen, ink and watercolor on watercolor paper, 8½" × 11" (22cm × 28cm)

Ardith Starostka, CDA, *The Enchanted Garden—Spring*, oil on pine cutout, 15¼″ × 11″ × 1″ (39cm × 28cm × 2.5cm)

6

EXPRESSIVE PORTRAITS

A face can be a storybook, a textbook or a drama full of emotions to be read in a quick glance or over the years. Our eyes are immediately attracted by any other pair in our view. Like magnets, eyes meet and acknowledge mutual presence.

Artists have painted faces and portraits since the very beginning of art history. Decorative painters are no exception, but the decorative painter chooses to show the best and brightest in the faces around them. The warm smile, the bright eye, the blush on the cheek attract the decorative painter.

Often the style employed by the decorative painter reflects the character of the subject in its straightforward simplicity. The next few pages show the extraordinary pleasure of painting portraits and faces.

ARDITH STAROSTKA, CDA

I enjoy designing pieces that depict young children and angels in the country/Victorian style. I collect old photographs from antique stores, catalogs and magazines, and also use pictures of my daughters Lindsay and Haley for inspiration. I like to design uniquely shaped pieces from pine, which I prefer because it is easy to cut and readily available at any lumberyard.

I first sanded and sealed the wood, then basecoated it with an ivory acrylic. After lightly tracing on the design, I misted the surface with Krylon Matte 1311. I use small amounts of oil paint on my brush to paint very thin layers, allowing the ivory basecoat to show through, creating highlights throughout the painting. I used variations of Brilliant Yellow Light, Vene-

tian Red and Thalo Yellow Green to mix the skin tones. I painted the hair with mixtures of Transparent Oxide Yellow and Raw Umber. To create the highlights in the hair, I lifted paint out with a small brush dampened with Winsor & Newton Blending and Glazing medium. I forced the drying time with two or three light coats of matte spray. I then reinforced my darkest areas and highlights and added details. To protect the finished piece, I used several light coats of matte spray.

Ardith Starostka, CDA, *The Enchanted Garden—Spring*, oil on pine cutout, 15¼″ × 11″ × 1″ (39cm × 28cm × 2.5cm)K × 1″

PAT CLARKE, MDA

I chose a bentwood box as the surface for my *Designing Women* idea because it has always been my favorite keepsake for unique and unusual momentoes of those special times in our lives, such as graduations, weddings, etc. In this piece I wanted to convey a strong design pattern on the top and side surfaces, connecting them with the band around the sides. By painting the women each of a different age and each facing a different direction, I added a bit of an oriental feel to the piece, possibly influenced by my recent teaching trip to Japan. Mixing black with the darkest warm tones used in the painting—Dioxazine Purple, Prussian Blue, Alizarin Crimson—gave me cool darks that help separate the different sections and elements within the design. My design was strengthened by the high contrast of these dark tones, along with the lightest lights which were used in limited areas, forming abstract shapes. The excitement of using the acrylics in a watercolor style allowed for much creativity and spontaneity on the sides of the box. Although I created interest on the sides of the box, I did not allow it to take away from the strongest focal area, the women on top of the box.

Pat Clarke, MDA, *Designing Women/Roses*, acrylic on bentwood box, 16″ × 10½″ × 9″ (41cm × 27cm × 23cm)

ATSUKO KURODA, CDA

This piece combines my two favorite painting subjects: portraits and flowers. The model is the daughter of my younger sister. My nieces are a great inspiration in my portraiture. I basecoated the wooden surface in blue-violet acrylic, then painted the portrait and flowers in oil, adding touches of yellow here and there to create complementary harmony. When I finished the painting, I felt the flowers were a bit "insistent," so I glazed over them with white oil, leaving a narrow band around the portrait untouched. The darker, unglazed area draws the focal point back to the portrait and creates a frame.

Glazing the flowers with white created another interesting effect: The flowers appear to be made of frosted glass, or covered with a layer of silk gauze. My final touch was to apply lettering in acrylic on the front cover and "spine" to make the box look like a book. I plan to present this piece to my niece when she is married, as a remembrance of her childhood.

Atsuko Kuroda, CDA, *Angel Story*, oil on book-shaped wooden box, 3½″ × 13″ × 15″ (8.8cm × 33cm × 38cm)

MICHELLE KERR, CDA

This piece was inspired by my mother's hand-sculpted jester creations. I wanted to pretend the jester was "on stage," hence the light coming in from the left and making his face and part of his collar the center of interest. I use Grumbacher MAX water-soluble oils. Although I don't use water with them, I like that they are nontoxic and odorless, but still feel like traditional oil paints. I like to mix my paints rather than using pre-mixed tube colors. I feel I get more intense and brilliant color this way. For this painting I chose my favorite color palette of violets, red-violets, pinks, blue-violets and yellow. I use Alizarin Crimson and French Ultramarine Blue to make my violets, and from there adjust to the red-violet or blue-violet side. When mixing any dark color on my palette, if I

can't tell which color it's leaning toward (e.g., red-violet or blue-violet), I place a small amount of the color on the side of my palette and add a tiny amount of white to it. For this painting I used a dry-brush blending technique: The paint is laid down and blended between values with only a small amount of paint loaded in the brush. I did the scrollwork and cross-hatching around the outside of the box with a liner brush and thinned gold acrylic paint. I finished the piece by spraying it with Blair Satin Tole.

Michelle Kerr, CDA, *Court Jester*, oil on oval bentwood box, 16″ × 6½″ × 4″ (41cm × 17cm × 10.1cm)

NANETTE RASBAND HILTON

The vivid, varied colors of the rainbow have always been my favorites. Happiness comes naturally when these bright colors surround me or play on the tip of my paintbrush. Often when I begin an illustration, I start with an inspirational quotation in mind and attempt to illustrate that thought. This piece comes from the saying, "We must each paint our own rainbow from the colors we've been given." By using a felt-tip, black-ink pen, I first create all the detailed lines of the illustration. Then, using small brushes and thin washes of paint, I gradually build up the color to the desired intensity. To finish my designs, I scatter "sunshine" throughout the illustration with

a subtle wash of bright yellow in the highlighted areas. Since I enjoy painting on functional pieces, this lap desk was an ideal (and inexpensive) surface. I figure that if the surface is one you'll use, you'll see and enjoy it more often. Since I tend to paint anything I think could be useful, that old joke about decorative artists painting anything that doesn't move keeps my husband quick on his feet!

Nanette Rasband Hilton, *Paint Your Own Rainbow*, acrylic pen and ink on wooden lap desk lid, 18″ × 14″ (46cm × 36cm)

TERRIE L. CORDRAY, CDA

While living in Utah, I drove back and forth to my home through many beautiful orchards of apples, peaches, pears and cherries. I loved the spring when the blossoms appeared, but most of all I looked forward to fall, when the fruit ripened and we could bring the sweet harvest home to make so many wonderful treats! When I came across this great tin piece, I thought it would make a terrific pie keep . . . but I'm sure it will be worthy of any yummy treat you can think of. The girls on the tin were inspired by my three beautiful daughters. This

tin came pre-primed, so all I needed to do was basecoat my background and begin to paint. I used the light background color for the highlights, then used various glazes of medium to dark values to create the overlay of color and shadows. To finish the piece, I varnished the tin with four coats of matte varnish and waxed it with beeswax.

Terrie L. Cordray, CDA, *Pie Makers Tin Keep*, acrylic gouache on tin, 11¼" (29cm) diameter

VI THURMOND, MDA

Portraits are my favorite subject matter to paint, and of all portrait subjects, I am especially fond of children dressed as clowns. This box was just the right size for a child to store tiny treasures in—from bits of ribbon, beads and buttons to cards and letters—so it lent itself well to the cheerful clown design. As I designed this piece, I knew I wanted the clown to be holding balloons, but had to come up with some way of attaching the balloons to an item which the clown would be holding. I thought of an umbrella (unopened) but finally decided on a cane, which would be easier to paint. My plan was to use a limited palette and make this project accessible to painters of any skill level. I do most of my portraits in oils, as they dry more slowly, allowing more time for blending. I have used acrylics on some smaller faces—with the use of extenders and a little practice you can get good blending.

Vi Thurmond, MDA, *Treasures*, oil on wooden book, 7″ × 1⅜″ × 8¼″ (18cm × 3.8cm × 21cm)

KIT STONER, CDA

I love to work on gourds, designing and painting a wide cast of characters according to the shape and size of each gourd. Often the shape of the gourd determines the personality it will become. *The Sea Captain* was designed for and resides in the private collection of two wonderful "seafaring" friends, one a former navy man. I love to personalize gourds with things that reflect an individual's personality, hence the addition of the maps, wheel, cat and wording on the captain's hat. I prepared the surface by scrubbing it with a Brillo pad and wire brush (using lots of elbow grease), then allowed it to dry well before beginning the painting. I drew the design on tracing paper that could be cut to fit the curved surface of the gourd. Often what looks good on flat paper has to be readjusted on the curved surface. Once I was satisfied with the elements of the design—such as the facial features and accessories in the character's hands—I began to paint. I first basecoated the face with Medium Flesh and the hat and coat areas with Liberty and Solider Blue acrylics. The patterns for the details were transferred to the gourd once the basecoat was dry. These design elements were basecoated a medium value, with shading and highlighting floated or drybrushed on. I use a building technique when shading and highlighting in this manner, often going back a number of times to further strengthen a light or dark area until I am happy with the effect. I added the detail work with a fine liner brush. The facial features were painted with Dark Flesh and developed in the same manner as the other details. I worked very carefully on the eyes, as I feel these lend much to the character's expressiveness. Once the face was completed, I added his beard and hair using a rake brush and different values of gray. When the paint was completely dry and cured, I sprayed the gourd with several coats of acrylic matte varnish to protect and seal the surface.

Kit Stoner, CDA, *The Sea Captain*, acrylic on natural gourd, 10″ × 16″ (25cm × 41cm)

Shirley Peterich, CDA, *Rosemaled Slavic Bowl in Rogaland Style,* acrylic gouache on wooden bowl, 14″ (36cm) diameter

7

TRADITIONAL STROKEWORK

Tradition is the repository of a community's discoveries and experience. It can never be lightly discarded. Contemporary decorative painting is built on the solid foundation of traditional folk painting. Much of it grows from the folk art traditions of Europe that were brought to North America by settlers from many countries.

This rich heritage has been a boundless resource for today's decorative painters. Many have preserved or revived the techniques of the Old World that would otherwise have disappeared. They have mastered (often by re-inventing lost procedures) the same skills once passed on from master to apprentice or from parent to child. Other artists have borrowed freely from the legacy of the past to invent new forms and new styles to create new traditions. Both are legitimate expressions of the decorative painters' creativity. Both are richly represented in the pages that follow.

SHIRLEY PETERICH, CDA

The colors for this bowl, painted with Jo Sonja's acrylics, were inspired by a bedspread in my daughter's home. The Rogaland style—named for the Rogaland county of Norway where it was created—is a form of the Norwegian folk art Rosemaling (meaning rose painting). I teach Rosemaling and other decorative arts in my home studio near Boise, Idaho. My husband, Don, makes all of my beautiful woodenware.

Shirley Peterich, CDA, *Rosemaled Slavic Bowl in Rogaland Style*, acrylic gouache on wooden bowl, 14″ (36cm) diameter

PAT VIRCH

The tine, pronouced *teena*, is constructed of thin wood bent under steam heat. The cover is held on by tension created by the two end wings. This is a very traditional piece of woodenware used frequently in the country home of the early 1800s. During the week it would hold Momma's knitting or needlework, and on Sunday it was packed with lunch to keep the kids quiet on the long, slow ride back home from church. Today I find this is the neatest way to take a pie or hot casserole to church potluck suppers. I have several of these unique boxes: one holds my small knitting projects by my easy chair, another holds all my painting supplies as I travel across the country teaching the lovely folk art of Norwegian rosemaling. Being of Norwegian blood lines has made me want to keep this folk art alive. I try to paint in styles that closely resemble the very old pieces found in museums and Norwegian homes today.

I based this tine with a low-lustre blue-black enamel. The scrolls are Yellow Ochre, shaded with Burnt Sienna. Good brush control is needed for Rosemaling, which is really just a combination of strokework and long, sweeping blending strokes. The Telemark style uses scrolls as a major part of the design. I used outlining work on a large percentage of the design. This type of outlining and accenting is not found in many other forms of European folk art. I used a burnt red shade to trim the tine and set the handle apart. This color also separates the two sides of the lid. To protect the painting, I finished the piece with varnish.

Pat Virch, *Norwegian Telemark Tine*, oil on bentwood box, 16″ (41cm) diameter × 6″ (15cm) depth

LYNDA DERBY

My students had been asking me for some time to create a design for a letter desk. Since this is such a functional piece, I wanted to design something that could go in almost any room of any home, and be used by a man or woman. For this reason I chose to do Norwegian Rosemaling. I wanted the color scheme to be dramatic and also had to chose design colors that would work on two different background colors, one inside and one on the outside. Although the bottom two panels on the inside of this desk come out for easier painting, I had a hard time basecoating the inside of the desk behind the third panel, which doesn't come out. I ended up using a cattail-shaped sponge brush to do the job, getting as much paint on me as on the piece!

Lynda Derby, *Rosemaling Letter Desk*, DecoArt acrylic on wooden letter desk, 14″ × 5″ × 11″ (36cm × 13cm × 28cm)

LYNNE DEPTULA

Fabric and wallpaper stores offer an endless supply of inspiration for decorative painters: There you can find the newest colors and themes and how they're being used. The flowers in this design were inspired by my favorite crewel-embroidery style fabrics and wallpapers. I have loved the bright colors and variety of stitches found in crewel embroidery since I was a high school student, planning on one day being a home economics teacher. After teaching for several years, I elected to stay home and raise a family. It was then that I discovered decorative painting. After a few lessons, I was hooked! (No needlecraft pun intended.) To paint the brightly colored flowers and leaves on this planter, I used the "soft floats" technique, a method of shading and highlighting that is easy to achieve and gives impressive results. I simply dampen a flower or leaf

with clear water, apply a wide layer of shade or highlight color, and let the water diffuse and soften the color out. When the color has dried completely, I repeat the procedure several more times until I achieve the desired depth of color. To protect painted tinware I first brush on a layer of acrylic varnish, making sure to get under the rim and along the seams to seal the piece completely. After the varnish has cured for twenty-four hours, I spray on an acrylic varnish spray to give the tinware a shiny finish. This piece allows me to enjoy the best of crewel embroidery and the best of decorative painting!

Lynne Deptula, *Strokework Sampler Planter*, acrylic on tin planter, 7½″ × 14″ (19cm × 36cm)

SHERRY GALL, CDA

Bauernmalerei (pronounced Bough-urn-mall-er-eye) translates as "farmer painting." It originates from the Alpine regions of Germany, Switzerland and Austria. Bauernmalerei is most easily recognized by its simplified flowers, the rose being the main symbol, along with the tulip, daisy, forget-me-not and other stylized flowers. I tried to incorporate these flowers in my design, although I paint in softer colors and give my flowers a more delicate look than the traditional style of this art form. I first sealed and then whitewashed the tray. Using a natural sea sponge, I lightly sponged the top with watery teal. I painted the design wet-on-wet using a no. 3 round brush. The flower colors—rose, peach, blue, yellow and lavendar—were inspired by thoughts of springtime.

Sherry Gall, CDA, *Bauernmalerei Vanity Tray*, acrylic on wooden tray with ball feet, 16″ × 6½″ × 2″ (41cm × 17cm × 5cm)

MELINDA NEIST

Having grown up on the east coast of Australia, I had always been attracted to anything made from shells. My father gave me a pearlshell bracelet which I treasured, and my grandmother taught me to make all kinds of ornaments using segments of polished shell. As I grew up, my fascination was directed toward the beautiful pearlshell inlay designs found on antiques, usually English, ranging from small boxes up to large furniture pieces. After moving to the United States, I discovered the wonderful acrylic metallic paints and set about to develop a technique to reproduce the look of realistic inlaid pearlshell.

The shell sections of this design are created by cutting a

stencil from "Stick n' Stencil," an adhesive film made by Visions. Using Accent Crown Jewel metallics, I apply a thick coat of Baroque Pearl and allow it to dry. I then apply patches of Empress Blue, Queen's Emerald, Dutchess Rose and Princely Pewter, softening each color with Baroque Pearl. When dry, I add veining, resembling that seen on polished abalone shell, by mixing Accent Real Black with Classical Bronze to produce an oyster brown. Next, I side load a round sable brush, stroke it out on a wet palette and float in the repetitive vein lines. I use Crown Jewel's Imperial Antique Gold for the line work to imitate the brass strip inlay that was

used to define the shape of the design and to create borders.

The floral designs on the box were painted using the single brush, multi-loading technique which is a very fast method of painting. In this method, several colors are loaded onto the brush at once and basecoat, highlight, shade and detail are created in the one stroke, using only one brush. For this technique I use the Accent Blending Colors line.

Melinda Neist, *Dome Box With Pearlshell Inlay*, acrylic on wooden trunk

DIANE EDWARDS

Rosemaling was done in Norway primarily in the 1700 and 1800s. Traditionally, it was done in gouache or tempera using dry pigments made from many different organic materials. Rosemaling has been revived in the last fifty years both in Norway and America, and is now done predominately in oils, although it can be done in a variety of media. The Rogaland style of Rosemaling—named for a county on the west coast of Norway in the Sand area—is a balanced, tightly painted style incorporating outlining and sharp edges, painted in traditional earth colors such as blues, rusts, dark greens and blacks.

I fell in love with Rosemaling in 1970 when my cousin Lynn and I visted Norway—the look of painted furniture and decorative walls in houses and churches was so beautiful, and so different from that of my prairie upbringing in North Dakota. This began my fascination with painting on old junk pieces and antiques that need some work. I find it very rewarding to create a work of art from something that others have discarded as junk. Rosemaling has become more than just a painting technique for me; it has become a way of life. Although it is a fairly difficult technique to master, I feel it is worth every minute to keep this beautiful art form alive.

Diane Edwards,
Rogaland Rosemaling—
Norwegian Corner
Cupboard, oil on
wooden corner
cupboard,
12″ × 12″ × 20″
(30cm × 30cm × 51cm)

PAT VIRCH

This wooden box is a reproduction of a very important piece found in rural Norwegian country homes in the eighteenth century. The family bible, all important papers and farm deeds were kept in such a box. It was usually displayed in the middle of the table, and therefore was decorated on all sides. I've decorated this box with a design from the Telemark district, using scrolls as the primary design motif. I painted it using a very limited color scheme of blue and yellow on a red background. I combined blue and Yellow Ochre to make the shades of green, and added some light accents with off-white. Outlining and overlay create the illusion of depth—light line work outlines the light side and black line work the dark side. Rather than varnish this piece, I finished it with paste wax, to which I added a small amount of black and Raw Umber oil color, creating an antiqued look. This is a good way to antique over acrylics, as the antiquing can be subdued by buffing, or removed completely by rubbing with fresh wax. If you decorate in oils, apply a coat of varnish to the surface before adding the wax to keep the oil color from lifting.

Pat Virch, *Norwegian Telemark Bible Box*, acrylic over latex enamel on wooden box, 9″ × 14″ × 6½″ (23cm × 36cm × 17cm)

Jill MacFarlane, *The List*, acrylic and oil on wooden cutout, 18″ × 11″ (46cm × 28cm)

8

CHRISTMAS CHEER

*J*ust as the Christmas season ends the year, so Christmas ends this volume of great decorative painting. And what a cheerful way to conclude it.

Of all the times of the year, Christmas is the most laden with memories and expectations. We look forward to the coming joys just as children anticipate the treasures to be found under the tree. We look back to all the Christmases past to relive and renew the happiness of those bygone times.

For the decorative painter, Christmas can be a year-round obsession. Decorative artists are planning, purchasing and painting Christmas items in every season. No sooner than the last ornament is packed away does the decorative painter begin to dream about next year.

The decorative painter cherishes all aspects of the holiday, from its religious foundation to Santa Claus and all the many popular customs. The range is wide and deep as this concluding chapter reveals in all its Yuletide splendor.

JILL MacFARLANE

A few years ago I decided that Santa should be portrayed as a real man. This decision took me on a long study of facial anatomy and expressions. You can see the results in this piece. It gives me great joy to have a child view my paintings and watch as a smile rises across his or her face. At this point I know I have achieved my goal.

Jill MacFarlane, *The List*, acrylic and oil on wooden cutout, 18″×11″ (46cm×28cm)

DEBRA COLE, CDA

It seems everyone loves teddy bears; however, I've been told I'm a teddy bear fanatic. The model for *Christmas Bear* is my favorite bear. He's an old, inexpensive, jointed bear whose fur is so worn and loose that he has folds in his cheeks. I love painting him because he has a lot of character. While designing this piece, I had a number of goals. One was to use a variety of textures to create interest in the design. I dug through my drawer of creative items—otherwise known as a junk drawer— and found an old tattered piece of rabbit fur. Copying its texture for the hatband created the softness within the design that I was looking for. My most important goal was to create a feeling of warmth and love. Mood is always my priority when designing; to get in the right mood to paint this piece, I reflected on the many blessings surrounding the Christmas season. I used DecoArt Americana and Delta Ceramcoat acrylics. I prefer pre-mixed bottled acrylics because I don't have to waste time mixing colors but can get right to the part I love,

painting the design. I use basic acrylic techniques such as floated color. I paint in stages, finishing all the first shades and highlights by building layers of semitransparent floats before going on to the second stage. I create form first, then add texture. I built up layers of texture in the fur by stippling, then combing, and finally lining the hairs. Using a Royal Golden Taklon series 730, ½-inch (12mm) comb brush made this process easier and faster; working with this brush is like using ten liner brushes at once. When the texture was complete, I added washes and glazes of colors from within the design; this step makes the bear come to life. My box is filled with the little treasures of Christmas that re-create the joy of the season.

Debra Cole, CDA, *Christmas Bear*, acrylic on wooden cheese box, 9″ (23cm) diameter

RITA M. MARTIN, CDA

When creativity is bubbling out of the top of my head, it's time to paint a gourd. The dried, hard-shelled fruits lend themselves well to just about any design, although my gourds are all centered around angels or Santas. The gourds are available in infinite sizes and shapes, offering an unobstructed surface with no predestined function. My sole intent is to produce something of elegant beauty from a mundane object. I purchase commercially grown dried gourds, clean and ready to paint. I choose each piece individually for its shape and clarity of surface. I painted *Angel Gourd* with acrylic paints and sponged some background areas. An abundance of strokework and beading provide interest over the entire piece. Folk-art roses and snowflakes repeat the colors of the angel, which is the center of interest. I finished the gourd with several coats of varnish to protect it.

Rita M. Martin, CDA, *Angel Gourd*, acrylic on natural dried gourd, 13″ × 8½″ (33cm × 22cm)

GRETCHEN CAGLE, CDA

Winter White and Colorful is a painting of true drama that defines the more elegant side of Christmas. The soft whiteness of the poinsettia is contrasted against the black background of the tray and then accented with a trim area of turquoise. The color is repeated in the ribbon and as accents on the flowers. Painting white flowers on a black background can be especially difficult since it is so hard to create an opaque white color against such a dark background. To overcome this problem, I added a bit of black oil color into the shading and tints areas of the flower; therefore, the background color becomes part of the painting, thus relating the two units together in complete harmony.

Gretchen Cagle, CDA, *Winter White and Colorful*, oil, alkyd and gold leaf on metal tray, 16″ (40.6cm)

CATHY SCHMIDT

I am a collector of many things, but my favorite objects to collect are Christmas ornaments. This round box gave me the perfect surface for my "Peace on Earth" theme. I really love the strong, bold colors. I stenciled the stars on and then tinted them with colors off my palette. I stippled the angels, then floated color on to softly blend the colors together. To give the stars more depth, I spattered the top surface and stars with warm white. I sealed the box with glaze medium and acrylic varnish, then waxed it for protection.

Cathy Schmidt, *Angel Toy Box,* acrylic on wooden box, 15″ (38cm) diameter

BARBARA NIELSEN, CDA

I loved this little heart-shaped sled the minute I saw it and knew I would paint a Santa on it. The design came easily, but I did spend some time deciding if Santa's free leg should be forward or back. I drew it both ways and decided on his foot forward; he was in a more level position, which looked better in the design. I first sealed and stained the sled, then based the top surfaces with several coats of white acrylic trimmed in blue. I based the ends of the runners and the three small hearts on the stained portion of the sled with the same blue. I then inked the design on the white area and added washes of acrylic over the inked drawing. I carefully based the sky around the design with two coats of black. My last touches were to re-ink some areas for sharpness, apply dots of acrylic and "pounce" snow on the trees and mountains with white. Before antiquing the piece with Burnt Umber oil paint, I sprayed it with acrylic spray to seal the ink lines. I then finished it with varnish.

Barbara Nielsen, CDA, *Santa Skating on Sled*, acrylic and pen and ink on wooden sled, 2″ × 6½″ × 12½″ (5cm × 17cm × 32cm)

TONI McGUIRE, CDA

In this piece, I combined my love of painting Santa with my love of painting on stoneware surfaces to create both a unique and functional Christmas keepsake. The stoneware coffeepot was unglazed on the outside surface, so it really needed no special preparation other than removing dust particles with a damp cloth before applying the pattern for the oval. I first basecoated the entire oval with black acrylic paint, then transferred the Santa pattern over the black surface with white graphite paper. I then basecoated the individual areas of the design with the appropriate colors. I did all of the shading and highlighting with a side-loaded flat brush and a floated color technique, in which several layers of color are floated on top of each other to create a gradation of value within the painting. I added a few highlights by drybrushing with a scruffy brush and a light value of paint. I always place special emphasis on the eyes when painting a face because I believe that when

the eyes sparkle, the entire face comes to life. I created the white beard, hair and mustache by basecoating these areas with a medium-value gray, then lining them with a liner brush and off-white paint to establish the direction in which the hair and beard grow. I gradually applied several layers of hair using the rake brush. Last, I added a few white lines to highlight the beard and give it added definition. I applied the strokework which decorates the spout and handle with black, then, using a small round brush, I overstroked it with gold. After the painting was completed, I sealed the outside surface by brushing on several coats of waterbased varnish.

Toni McGuire, CDA, *Coffee With Santa*, acrylic on stoneware, 10″ × 6½″ × 8½″ (25cm × 17cm × 22cm)

GLORIA KOSKEY, MDA

This cabinet's primitive, country style prompted me to design a St. Nicholas with a "backwoods" feel. To complement this theme, I framed the design with twigs on the door panel and around the holly and ivy trim on the top. I first basecoated the entire cabinet with a medium-value moss green acrylic. I then used a dry-brush technique and a lighter color to create an interesting effect on the surface. Next I antiqued the design area with a mixture of oil paint and medium; the antiquing creates the shadows and dark areas in the design. In areas of the design where highlights would appear, I rubbed the antiquing off. I added the light values with oil colors, using the paint sparingly, with a quite dry-brush. After adding the holly and ivy trim, I antiqued and highlighted these areas with oils, keeping the highlights minimal so the trim didn't compete with the main design area. I finished the remainder of the cabinet with the antiquing mixture, leaving it dark around the edges and lighter in the center of the sides and on the doorframe.

Gloria Koskey, MDA, *North Woods St. Nicholas*, oil over acrylic on wooden cabinet, 6½″ × 10″ × 18″ (17cm × 25cm × 46cm)

PEGGY HARRIS

I *love* holidays! Holidays are giant creative magnets to the decorative artist in me. I'm helpless to resist their pull. Small matter that I've only got a few days to create a "masterpiece" for friends and loved ones to "hand down for generations." Consequently, what I envisioned as an annual limited edition of one hundred Christmas balls shrank to twenty the first year, less each succeeding year, and now has dwindled to two a year—one for my daughter and one for a dear friend. But the tradition is established and somehow it just wouldn't be Christmas without painting Christmas balls.

Frosted glass is the easist surface to work on, but white porcelain is very attractive also. Most surfaces will be easier to paint if they are lightly sprayed with a sealer. The cardboard ring from inside a roll of masking or shipping tape makes a safe and convenient holder while painting and drying the ball. Whether painting with acrylics or oils, use a wet-on-wet technique and a gel medium to hold the brushmarks that create

the soft, fluffy look of the feathers. Lightly rake a stiff bristle or sable filbert brush which has been moistened in gel medium through the base paint. Use Q-tips to remove color from highlighted areas, add white paint and then blend the white into the surrounding color with a bristle brush. If you're working in oils, a touch of a commercial drier in your paint will have your ornament ready in time for Santa. Snowflakes are best painted in acrylic since it dries rapidly and allows you to turn and handle the ball as you work. After protecting the ball with an appropriate sealer, personalize and sign it on the back with a gold pen. Imagine a tree filled with your Christmas balls and a small child saying, "My great-great-great-great grandmother painted these for *me*!"

Peggy Harris, *Joy to the World* (cardinal) and *Heaven and Nature Sing* (chickadee), oil and acrylic on frosted glass ornament, 3¼″ (7.7cm) diameter

JOYCE MORRISON

My goal in planning this project was to create an heirloom-quality skirt which combined my two favorite painting subjects: realistic florals and Rosemaling. I designed the poinsettias and scrolls in a symmetrical pattern, incorporating the cutwork and embroidered design on the beautiful Battenburg lace skirt. I first mounted the skirt on a fabric painting board and covered the excess fabric with plastic to protect the white surface. I used a wet-on-wet technique to apply the fabric paints, completing one section totally before moving to another. I base painted, shaded and added the first highlight with So-Soft paint. I added the second and third highlights with Shimmer-ing Pearls paint—the touch of glitter in this paint added a subtle sparkle to these highlights. I did the line work on the scrolls with metallic gold. This was not a quick or simple project, but the end results were well worth the time invested. Current and future generations will look at this skirt with pride, seeing something of the creative person who painted this heirloom for them to enjoy.

Joyce Morrison, *Poinsettia Christmas Tree Skirt*, DecoArt So-Soft and Shimmering Pearls fabric acrylics on Battenburg lace skirt, 72″ (183cm) diameter

AILEEN L. BRATTON, CDA

I painted these Christmas ornaments for a very special Christmas tree, which I display in our bedroom. I chose a floral design because I love flowers and elegant themes. The ornaments are trimmed with gold leaf. I added the final details and stronger highlights and shadows with a glazing technique. I then varnished the ornaments and, when dry, applied wax with very fine steel wool, giving the ornaments a warm glow.

Aileen L. Bratton, CDA, *Christmas With a Touch of Class*, alkyd, oil and gold leaf on porcelain ornaments, 4½″ (11.4cm) diameter

Contributors

The artists whose addresses are listed below encourage you to contact them for information on other publications, pattern packets, workshops and classes. Those artists whose listings include "Pattern available" are offering pattern packets for the exact piece featured in this book. Contact the artist directly to order these patterns, or for more information. To order other North Light books mentioned below, call (800) 289-0963. All prices are in U.S. currency unless otherwise noted. Please do not send cash. North Light Books is not responsible for the sales, shipping or quality of these patterns.

JO ALLAN, 2904 Blakiston Dr. NW, Calgary, Alberta T2L 1L6 Canada; phone: (403) 282-9104; p. 37 *Bronze Poppies* © Jo Allan.

SHARON ARCHER, CDA, 1576 Verona Pitsburg Rd., Arcanum, OH 45304; phone: (937) 884-7103; p. 88 *Country Winter Sled* © Sharon Archer. Pattern available for $10, including shipping and handling.

MARLENE BARKER, CDA, PO Box 144, Hot Sulphur Springs, CO 80451; phone: (970) 725-3608; p. 39 *Springtime Blessings* © Marlene Barker. Pattern available for $4.50.

JANE BARRIENTOS, CDA, 33 Cooper St., West Springfield, MA 01089; phone: (413) 736-8882; p. 76 *Cherries and Nuts* © Jane Barrientos. Pattern available for $8.50 plus $1.50 postage and handling.

MARY L. BEAN, 2927 N. 81st Ave., Phoenix, AZ 85033; phone: (602) 849-1382; p. 25 *Sweet Peas* © Mary L. Bean. Information on other pattern packets available by request.

TRUDY BEARD, Trudy Beard Publications, 121 Calvin Park Blvd., Rockford, IL 61107; phone: (815) 229-2393; fax: (815) 227-9646; p. 26 *Aunt Ida's Tulips* © Trudy Beard. Pattern available for $9.95 plus $1.25 postage and handling. Send check or money order. No credit cards.

ARLENE BECK, MDA, 3255 Scotch Ridge Rd., Duanesburg, NY 12056; phone: (518) 895-8937; p. 18 *Sunlit Roses* © Arlene Beck. Techniques for creating beautiful, realistic flowers like these are taught in Arlene's book, *Painting Realistic Flowers in Acrylic*, published by North Light Books.

DIANE BEGGINES-PHALEN, Diane Phalen Watercolors, PO Box 820, Banks, OR 97106; phone: (800) 832-3463, local calls (503) 324-1108); fax: (503) 324-3463; e-mail: dpwc@teleport.com; website: http://www.teleport.com/~dpwc/; p. 84 *Summer Memories* © Diane Beginnes-Phalen. Write to the above address for a free brochure of Diane's prints and gift items. Full color step-by-step instructions for many other charming country scenes are featured in Diane's new North Light book, *Painting the American Heartland in Watercolor*.

AILEEN L. BRATTON, CDA, 11215 Inverness Ct. NE, Albuquerque, NM 87111-7547; phone: (505) 298-2222; fax: (505) 298-2121; e-mail: aileenvt@aol.com; p. 139 *Christmas With a Touch of Class* © Aileen Bratton. Step-by-step instructions for other classic floral and fruit designs appear in Aileen's new North Light compilation, *Aileen Bratton's Decorative Painting Treasures*.

AVIS BRAUN, CDA, 5008 Hwy. 64, Pound, WI 54161; phone: (414) 897-3945; p. 43 *Tulip Time* © Avis Braun. Pattern available for $6.00 plus $1.25 shipping.

SHARON BUONONATO, CDA, 134 Slate Quarry Rd., Rhinebeck, NY 12572; phone; (914) 266-5678; e-mail: SHARONBSORIGINALS@worldnet.att.net; p. 85 *Catskill Autumn* © Sharon Buononato. Pattern available for $7. Wholesale orders available.

CAROL-LEE CISCO, CDA, Classical Expressions, 1309 Dunbarton Dr., Richardson, TX 75081; phone: (972) 690-9218; fax: (972) 783-0819; pp. 70-71 *Getting Organized* © Carol-Lee Cisco. Pattern available for $10 plus $2 shipping and handling.

PAT CLARKE, MDA, The Country Saltbox, 21714 S. Mulberry Hill Rd., Pleasant Hill, MO 64080; phone: (816) 540-2874; fax: (816) 987-2100; p. 107 *Designing Women/Roses* © Pat Clarke. Pattern available for $12.00 plus $3.50 shipping and handling. Catalog of publications, over 100 packets, books and videos available for $5.00 plus $3.50 postage. Also look for Pat's new North Light book *Painting Portraits with Acrylics*, due out in the fall of 1999.

SANDRA S. CODDAIRE, CDA; 14 Noblewood Place, Willingboro, NJ 08046; phone: (609) 871-6428; e-mail: scoddair@erols.com; p. 79 *Hoosier School Days* © Sandra S. Coddaire. Pattern available for $6.50 (includes postage).

DEBRA COLE, CDA, Heaven Sent Publications, 799 Lancelot Lane, Collierville, TN 38017; p. 129 *Christmas Bear* © Debra Cole. Pattern available for $6.99 plus $2.00 shipping and handling. Visa/MasterCard accepted.

TERRIE L. CORDRAY, CDA, Opinery Folk Art Studio, PO Box 7169, Cross Lanes, WV 25356; fax: (304) 776-7883; e-mail: opinery@citynet.net; website: http://www.citynet.net/opineryfolkart; p. 111 *Pie Makers Tin Keep* © Terrie L. Cordray. Pattern available for $12.50, including shipping and handling. Information on local and travel teaching seminars available by request.

BILL DeLOACH, Oils by Bill DeLoach, Inc., 901 Wilson Street, West Monroe, LA 71291; phone: (888) 324-OILS (toll free); e-mail: obbd@bayou.com; website: http://www.bayou.com/obbd; p. 83 *Grandma's Knitting Box* © Bill DeLoach. Pattern available for $5. Visa/MasterCard accepted.

CHERI DENNETT, 20 Bartlett Rd., Brentwood, NH 03833; fax: (603) 778-8131; e-mail: CheriD7777@aol.com; p. 58 *Cherries in China* © Cheri Dennett. Pattern available for $6.50 plus $1.00 shipping.

DOROTHY DENT, Painter's Corner, Inc., 108 W. Hwy. 174, Republic, MO 65738; phone: (417) 732-2076; fax: (417) 732-1127; website: http://www.bayou.com/obbd/dent/;

pp. 80-81, 82 *Summer Evening* © Dorothy Dent. Pattern available for $8.00 plus $1.25 shipping and handling.

LYNNE DEPTULA, 7245 Cascade Wds. Dr. SE, Grand Rapids, MI 49546; phone: (616) 940-1899; fax: (616) 940-6002; p. 120 *Strokework Sampler Platter* © Lynne Deptula. Pattern available for $8 including shipping and handling.

LYNDA DERBY, The Painting Derby, 5 Carleton Rd., Mont Vernon, NH 03057; phone/fax: (603) 673-0744; e-mail: donlyn@donlyn.mv.com; pp. 118-119 *Rosemaling Letter Desk* © Lynda Derby. Pattern available for $8 plus shipping and handling.

PATTI J. DeRENZO, CDA, DeRenzo's Designs, PO Box 3385, Crestline, CA 92325; phone: (909) 338-2215; p. 72 *Thy Word is a Lamp Unto My Feet* © Patti J. DeRenzo. Pattern available for $8.00 plus $1.50 shipping and handling.

DONNA DEWBERRY, 811 E. Highland Dr., Altamonte Springs, FL 32701, phone: (407) 830-6786; fax: (407) 831-0658; website: www.onestroke.com, p. 33 *Rose Bouquet Serving Tray* © Donna Dewberry. Pattern available from above address for $7.95. Also look for Donna's new North Light book, *Donna Dewberry's Complete Book of One-Stroke Painting.*

JUDY DIEPHOUSE, 1674 Hall SE, Grand Rapids, MI 49506; phone: (616)-241-2937; fax: (616) 241-4766; e-mail: DistinctJ@aol.com; pp. 74-75 *Italian Dinner Spice Cabinet With Holiday Insert* © Judy Diephouse.

RUTH DOLSEN, 7916 Magnolia, Brighton, MI 48116-1330; phone: (810) 227-5545; p. 86 *Americana Basket* © Ruth Dolsen. Pattern available for $7 plus $1 shipping and handling. Flyer available upon request with SASE.

JUDY DUARTE, PO Box 832, La Verkin, Utah 84745; p. 45 *Victorian Foot Stool* © Judy Duarte. Pattern available for $6.95. Foot stool available from Wood Chuck Ind., 36420 Calle Puerta Bonita, Temecula, CA 92599.

DIANE EDWARDS, 219 Driftwood Place, Alamosa, CO 81101; phone: (719) 587-0207 (h), (719) 589-3308 (w); fax: (719) 589-3676; p. 124 *Rogaland Rosemaling—Norwegian Corner Cupboard* © Diane Edwards. Pattern available for $10 plus postage. Visa/MasterCard and Discover cards accepted.

GINGER EDWARDS, 2136 Memorial Dr., Alexandria, LA 71301; phone: (318) 448-8726; fax: (318) 443-4473; p. 16 *Old Fashioned Elegance* © Ginger Edwards.

DOROTHY EGAN, 1343 E. 19th, Tulsa, OK 74120; phone/fax: (918) 743-7187; p. 99 *Canada Goose Desk Caddy* © Dorothy Egan. This pattern can be found in Dorothy's book, *Take Another Gander,* available for $9.95 plus $2.00 postage and handling. Also look for Dorothy's two North Light books, *Painting and Decorating Birdhouses* and *How to Start Making Money With Your Decorative Painting.*

CAROL EMPET, CDA, Fruit n' Flower Art, 983 West Dryden Rd., Freeville, NY 13068-9743; phone: (607) 257-1820; p. 46 *Gathering Basket* © Carol Empet. Pattern available for $10.50 plus $1.50 shipping and handling. The wooden cutout can be ordered for $10 plus $2 shipping and handling. NY residents please include 8% sales tax on all orders.

CINDY FORSYTHE, MDA, 7506 Pine Green Lane, Humble, TX 77346; phone/fax: (281) 852-4831; p. 21 *Lady's Hanging Tool Chest With Hibiscus.* Pattern available for $7.00 plus $1.25 shipping and handling.

DEANNE FORTNAM, MDA, 18 Cambridge Rd., Nashua, NH 03062; phone: (603) 889-1434; fax: (603) 881-3579; pp. 10-11, 12 *Clematis and Yellow Roses* © Deanne Fortnam. Full color step-by-step instructions and pattern available for this and many other beautiful rose designs in Deanne's new North Light book, *Painting Roses With Deanne Fortnam MDA.*

SHERRY GALL, CDA, 22851 Wind Song Place, Canyon Lake, CA 92587; phone/fax: (909) 244-3837; e-mail: rong@pe.net; p. 121 *Bauernmalerei Vanity Tray* © Sherry Gall. Pattern available for $6 plus $2 shipping.

LOIS GIVEN, 2982 S. Newport St., Denver, CO 80224; p. 89 *Welcoming Committee* © Lois Given. Pattern available for $10. Please write for a brochure and price list for the *Highlands & Hedgerows* books and packets.

JEANIE T. GROVES, Silk' n Things, 1220 Edgewood Ave. Las Cruces, NM 88005; phone: (505) 524-1018; e-mail: silknthings@zianet.com; website: www.zianet.com\silknthings; p. 24 *Summer Splendor Pillow Top* © Jeanie T. Groves. Pattern available for $7.50 prepaid.

ANN GRZYMSKI, CDA, 70 Elmwood Dr., Apalachin, NY 13732; phone: (607) 625-2433; p. 47 *Pansy Box* © Ann Grzymski. Pattern available for $5.00, plus $.50 postage and handling. NY State residents add 8% sales tax.

JOHN GUTCHER, 1001 Morrison Ct., Tampa, FL 33629-4912; phone: (813) 289-4479; fax: (813) 251-2321; pp. 94-95 *Peacock and Trompe L'Oeil Feather* © John Gutcher. Pattern available for $20. Other patterns, videos and travel teaching information available upon request.

PEGGY HARRIS, P.O. Box 784, Antioch, TN 37011; p. 137 *Joy to the World* and *Heaven and Nature Sing* © Peggy Harris. Patterns available from above address for $8 per ornament. Please specify which design you are ordering. For information on seminars and workshops, contact Swanson International at (800) 251-1402. For complete step-by-step illustrations on painting other darling baby animals, look for Peggy's North Light books, *Painting Baby Animals With Peggy Harris* and *Painting More Baby Animals.*

PRISCILLA HAUSER, MDA, P.O. Box 521013, Tulsa, OK 74152; phone: (918) 743-6072; fax: (918) 743-5075; e-mail: PHauser376@aol.com; website: http://fallriver.ns.ca/hauser, p. 4-5, 27 *A Celebration of Roses* © Priscilla Hauser. Pattern and full color, step-by-step instructions and worksheets for these roses and many other beautiful flowers can be found in *Priscilla Hauser's Book of Decorative Painting,* available from North Light books. Seminar information available by request to the above address.

BETTY HERRON, CDA, Unique Arts, 3394 Woodsdale Rd., Salem, OH 44460; phone: (330) 222-1667; p. 61 *Wreath of Fruit* © Betty Herron. Pattern available for $6 plus $1 shipping and handling ($2 outside U.S.) Visa/MasterCard and American Express accepted.

NANETTE RASBAND HILTON, 2810 Micah Ave., Henderson, NV 89014; phone: (702) 896-4359 or (702) 260-9151; p. 110 *Paint Your Own Rainbow* © Nanette Rasband Hilton. Pattern available for $8.95 from Eas'l Publishing, PO Box 22088, St. Louis, MO 63126-0088; phone: (314)-892-9222.

ENID HOESSINGER, CDA, PO Box 5540, Cairns 4870, North Queensland, Australia; phone: 61-70-341106; fax: 61-70-41865; pp. 14-15 *Say it With Flowers* © Enid Hoessinger. Full color step-by-step instructions for a variety of folk art flowers are featured in Enid's new decorative painting book, to be published by North Light books in the Spring of 1999.

CATHERINE HOLMAN, 103 Lakeview Drive, Excelsior Springs, MO 64024; phone: (816) 630-5832; e-mail: CAHOLMAN1@aol.com; p. 87 *Village of Stoney Point* © Catherine Holman. This and other patterns can be found in the book *Village of Stoney Point*, available from the above address for $9.95 plus $1.50 shipping and handling. A free catalog is also available upon request with a business-size SASE. Look for Catherine's new book on painting country villages, to be published by North Light books in the Fall of 1999.

LOUISE JACKSON, MDA, 1341 Yankee Vineyards, Centerville, OH 45458; phone: (937) 291-9184; fax: (937) 291-9084; p. 64 *Red Apples* © Louise Jackson. Pattern available for $13. Also look for Louise's new North Light book, *Painting Flowers in Watercolor With Louise Jackson.*

CHARLES JOHNSON, Designs From Charles Johnson, Box 4092 GSS, Springfield, Missouri 65808; phone: (417) 887-5524; pp. 40-41 *Victorian Keepsake Box* © Charles Johnson. Pattern available for $8.50.

ANDY B. JONES, CDA, PCM Studios, 731 Highland Ave. NE, Suite D, Atlanta, GA 30312; phone/fax: (404) 222-0348; p. 20 *Single Orchid* © Andy B. Jones.

DOXIE A. KELLER, 127 West 30th, Hutchinson, KS 67502; phone: (316) 665-6256; e-mail: doxie@southwind.net; website: http:www.tolenet.com/doxie/; p. 30 *Pastel Dimensional Flowers—Easy Does It* © Doxie A. Keller. Pattern available for $5. For orders outside the U.S. please send postal money orders or Visa/MasterCard number

and expiration date. The bombay box is available from Valhalla Designs, 343 Twin Pines Dr., Glendale, OR 97442.

MICHELLE KERR, CDA, 157 Elsbree Circle, Windsor, CA 95492; phone/fax: (707) 838-3675 (h); phone/fax: (707) 838-3152 (w); e-mail: Vepaint@aol.com; p. 109 *Court Jester* © Michelle Kerr. Pattern available for $8.50 plus $1.00 shipping and handling. Other related items available by request.

GLORIA KOSKEY, MDA, Americana Sampler Designs, 3434 So. 114th E. Ave, Tulsa, OK 74146; phone: (918) 627-8876; p. 136 *North Woods St. Nicholas* © Gloria Koskey. Pattern available for $6.50 plus $2.00 postage and handling. For orders outside the U.S., please send postal money order in U.S. currency. Wooden cabinet available from Country Pleasures, HCR #64, Box 53, Thayer, MO 65791. (417) 264-7246.

ATSUKO KURODA, CDA, 13-46-703 Asahigaoka-cho, Ashiya City, Hyogo 659, Japan; phone/fax: 81-797-38-1503; p. 108 *Angel Story* © Atsuko Kuroda.

DeLANE LANGE, 2206 E. Farm Rd. 188, Ozark, MO 65721; phone: (417) 887-8717; fax: (417) 887-5293; e-mail: delane@~csi.-net; p. 102 *Anniversary Trunk* © DeLane Lange. The pattern for this project appears in the book *Victorian Flowers and More*, available from the above address for $10.95. Also look for DeLane's new book *Painting Decorative Heirlooms with Delane Lange* to be published by North Light books in the Spring of 1999.

DOLORES LENNON, MDA, 1626 E. Kathleen Rd., Phoenix, AZ 85022; phone: (602) 485-9180; p. 19 *Alaina's Roses* © Dolores Lennon. Pattern available for $7.50 plus $2.50 shipping and handling. Please send check at time of order. Pattern will be shipped asap.

A. JOAN LOCKYEAR, CDA, 19 Kenwood Crescent, London, Ontario, Canada N5Y 3W6; p. 78 *Canadian Breakfast* © A. Joan Lockyear. Pattern available for $10.

JILL MacFARLANE, 13457 88th Ave. N., Seminole, FL 33772; phone: (813) 393-8870; pp. 126-127, 128 *The List* © Jill Macfarlane. Pattern available for $6. Wooden cutout and brushes also available.

RITA M. MARTIN, CDA, 4176 East 350 North, Rolling Prairie, IN 46371; phone: (219) 778-4638; pp. 130-131 *Angel Gourd* © Rita M. Martin. Painted gourds available for purchase, by appointment only.

MARY McCULLAH, CDA, 5101 Foxfire Trail, Kingsport, TN 37664; Voicemail: (423) 288-9688; fax: (423) 288-8573; p. 101 *Berry Patch Beauty—Askina* © Mary McCullah. Pattern available for $9.95 plus $2.00 shipping and handling. Send legal-size SASE for a catalog of other available pattern packets.

TONI McGUIRE, CDA, 4801 Jeffery Lane, Paducah, KY 42001; phone: (502) 554-5811; pp. 134-135 *Coffee With Santa* © Toni McGuire. Pattern available for $8 postage paid.

MARY McLEAN, CDA, 10 Sharon Ave., Norfolk, MA 02056; e-mail: Mcleanmdl @aol.com; pp. 50-51, 52 *Glorious Fruit* © Mary McLean. Pattern available for $9. Please request pattern #143 Glorious Fruit.

BRENDA McPEEK, CDA, 8915 Maple Dr., Overland Park, KS 66207; phone: (913) 649-2082; pp. 66-67, 68 *Graniteware and Blueberries* © Brenda McPeek. Pattern available for $10.

KARL-HEINZ MESCHBACH, CGCDP, "The Faux Meister," 4901—106th Ave. NE, Circle Pines, MN 55014; phone: (612) 785-2533; p. 93 *Birds of a Feather* © Karl-Heinz Meschbach. Pattern available for $14.85.

AUDREY D. MITCHELL, CDA (MDA Floral), 1435 Goldthorpe Rd., Mississauga, Ontario L5G 3R2 Canada; phone: (905) 274-7280; fax: (905) 278-4778; p. 42 *Blended Rose on Magazine Holder* © Audrey D. Mitchell. Pattern available for $6.25 ($8.50 Canadian) plus $ .50 postage. Includes instructions for both oils and acrylics.

JO AVIS MOORE, MDA, 4005 E. 80th St., Tulsa, OK 74136-8036; phone: (918) 496-2254; fax: (918) 496-2187; p. 48 *A Plate With Roses and Plums* © Jo Avis Moore

JOYCE MORRISON, 14718 Cape Dr., E., Jacksonville, FL 32226; phone: (904) 751-4518; fax: 904-757-2058; p. 138 *Poinsettia Christmas Tree Skirt* © Joyce Morrison. Pattern available for $7.50. Please request packet # 0019 PTS—Poinsettia Christmas Tree Skirt.

LuANNE MURPHY, 1709 W. Latoka, Springfield, Missouri 65807; phone: (417) 865-7301; p. 98 *Spirit Wolf* © LuAnne Murphy. Pattern available for $8.50 plus $2.75 shipping and handling. MO residents add 6.1% sales tax.

PHILLIP C. MYER, PCM Studios, 731 Highland Avenue NE, Suite D, Atlanta, GA 30312-1425; phone/fax: (404) 222-0348; e-mail: abjpcm@aol.com; p. 34 *A Blooming Rose* © Phillip C. Myer. Pattern available for $9.95. Books, videos, brushes and seminar information available by request. Also look for Phillip's four North Light books, *Creative Paint Finishes for Furniture, Creative Paint Finishes for the Home, Painting and Decorating Cabinets & Chests* and *Painting & Decorating Frames.*

BARBARA A. NEFF, 205 E. Glisson, Electra, TX 76360-1920; phone: (940) 495-2025 or (940) 495-3093; p. 38 *Dark Night Iris* © Barbara A. Neff. Pattern available for $6.00 plus $2.50 shipping and handling.

MELINDA NEIST, PO Box 726, Queanbeyan 2620, N.S.W. Australia; fax: 06 280 6673; e-mail: 100 243.553@compuserve.com; pp. 122-123 *Dome Box With Pearlshell Inlay and Multi-Loading Technique* © Melinda Neist. Pattern available for $6 from Valhalla Designs, 343 Twin Pines Dr., Glendale, OR 97442.

SHERRY C. NELSON, MDA, PO Box 530, Portal, AZ 85632; phone/fax: (520) 558-2285; pp. 90-91, 92 *A Touch of Gold—Yellow Warbler* © Sherry C. Nelson. Pattern available for $5 plus $1 shipping and handling. Sherry teaches step-by-step techniques for painting a variety of realistic birds in her new book, *Painting Garden Birds With Sherry C. Nelson, MDA,* from North Light books.

CLAUDIA NICE, p. 103 *Rabbit in the Blackberry Brambles* © Claudia Nice. This project appears in the book *Scenes From Seasons Past.* The book can be ordered for $12 from Susan Scheewe Publications, Inc., 13435 NE Whitaker Way, Portland, OR 97230. (503) 254-9100. Also look for Claudia's four North Light books, including her newest, *Painting Nature in Pen, Ink & Watercolor.*

BARBARA NIELSEN, CDA, 1259 Bedford St., Fremont, CA 94539; phone: (510) 656-8173; fax: (510) 656-5722; p. 133 *Santa Skating on Sled* © Barbara Nielsen. Pattern available for $5 plus $1 postage and handling.

TINA SUE NORRIS, Tina Designs, PO Box 148, Perry, OH 44081; phone: (216) 259-3580; p. 73 *Leaf Collector's Box* © Tina Sue Norris. Pattern available for $5.50. Please request pattern #TT 104. Catalog available for $3. Seminar information available upon request.

PEGGY NUTTALL; p. 54 *Spray of Apples* © Peggy Nuttall. Similar designs can be found in volumes I, II and III of Peggy's latest decorative painting book series, *An Old Fashioned Garden.*

JACKIE O'KEEFE, 1290 St. George Rd., Merritt Island, FL 32952-6112; phone: (407) 452-4100; p. 32 *Family Records* © Jackie O'Keefe. This pattern can be found in Jackie's book, *Personal Collection Part II,* published by Viking Folk Art Publications. The book is available for $9.95. Also look for Jackie's new North Light book, *Handlettering for Decorative Artists.*

PAT PARKER, Tomorrow's Heirlooms, 2085 Cook Rd., Charlton, NY 12019; phone/fax (call first): (518) 882-9099; e-mail: THeirlooms@aol.com; p. 29 *Spring Floral Wreath* © Pat Parker. Pattern available for $7.50 plus $1.50 shipping for one packet, $2.00 shipping for two or more packets. NY state residents add 7% state sales tax.

GLORIA PERKINS, 236 Craig Wood Way, Sharpsburg, GA 30277; phone: (770) 463-3300; p. 49 *Grandmother's Roses* © Gloria Perkins. Pattern available for $12, including tax and postage.

SHIRLEY PETERICH, CDA, Shirley's Studio, 540 N. Harvey Lane, Eagle, ID 83616; phone: (208) 939-6753; pp. 114-115, 116 *Rosemaled Slavic Bowl in Rogaland Style* © Shirley Peterich. Pattern available for $8. Bowl (14″ diameter) available for $30. Both prices include postage and handling.

CAROLYN L. PHILLIPS, 5416 Temple City Blvd., Temple City, CA 91780-3150; phone: (818) 285-4341; fax: (818) 285-5548; e-mail: CarolynPhi@aol.com; p. 53 *Apple and Pear Plate* © Carolyn L. Phillips Pattern available for $7 plus $2 shipping. Write or call for information on books, pattern packets and seminars.

SUE PRUETT, MDA, 3761 Stanford Dr., Oceanside, CA 92056; phone/fax: (760) 721-1671; p. 28 *Cheri's Rose* © Sue Pruett. Pattern available for $7.95.

SUSIE SAUNDERS, The Heart of Byfield, 1 Lunt St., Byfield, MA 01922; phone: (508) 465-8026; fax: (508) 465-5273; p. 60 *Early American Fruit Cupboard* © Susie Saunders. Pattern available for $6 plus $1 postage.

CATHY SCHMIDT, Cat's Studio, 19302 S. Fernwood Rd., Molalla, OR 97038; phone: (503) 829-3685; p. 132 *Angel Toy Box* © Cathy Schmidt. Pattern available for $6.00 plus $.75 postage.

PEGGI SEVERINI, CDA, Box 5428, Woodland Park, CO 80866; phone: (719) 687-9491; e-mail: lilbrush@aol.com; p. 17 *Columbines and Old Lace* © Peggi Severini. Pattern available for $6.50 plus $2.00 shipping and handling. Catalog available upon request.

JACKIE SHAW, 13306 Edgemont Rd., Smithsburg, MD 21783; phone: (301) 824-6509; website: www.jackieshaw.com; pp. 22-23 *A Family of Love* © Jackie Shaw. Pattern, step-by-step instructions and worksheets for this project can be found in *The Big Book of Decorative Painting,* 336 pages. Available for $35.00 plus $4.50 postage and handling from KG Services (Jackie Shaw Mail Order Dept.), 733 Peaks St., Bedford, VA 24523.

LESLIE SMITH, CDA, 263 Woodlands Rd., Lake Worth, FL 33461; p. 77 *Just an Old Fashioned Nosegay* © Leslie Smith. Pattern available for $13.95 plus shipping and handling.

VIRGINIA SMITH, CDA, 344 Garden Dr.; Wintersville, OH 43952; phone: (614) 264-1097; p. 62 *Mixed Fruit* © Virginia Smith. Pattern available for $7.

JANET G. SNELL, The Decorative Art Works, 1273 Pembroke Ct, Schenectady, NY 12309; phone: (518) 382-0647; fax: (518) 382-0920; e-mail: JSNELLDAW@aol.com; p. 69 Red, *White and Blue Recipe Box* © Janet G. Snell. Pattern available for $6.00 plus $1.50 shipping. NY state residents add 7% sales tax.

HELEN STADTER, MDA, 1200 W. 30th St. S., Independence, MO 64055; phone: (816) 254-4223; p. 35 *Roses Run Wild* ©

Helen Stadter. Pattern available for $5.

SHARON STANSIFER, CDA, 20661 Porter Ranch Rd., Trabuco Canyon, CA 92679; phone/fax: (714) 589-2571; p. 96 *Sleepy Baby Bobcats* © Sharon Stansifer. Pattern available for $7.95 plus shipping. Other wildlife designs available by request. Look for Sharon's new North Light Book, *Basic Brushstrokes for Decorative Painting*, due Fall 1999.

ARDITH STAROSTKA, Star Studio Arts, 31 Clear Lake, Columbus, NE 68601; phone: (402) 564-1801; fax: (402) 564-9844; e-mail: rstrakt@megavision.com; pp. 104-105, 106 *The Enchanted Garden— Spring* © Ardith Starostka.

BRENDA STEWART, CDA, 11825 Blandfield St., Richmond, VA 23233; phone/fax (804) 364-1924; p. 55 *Nature's Bounty Spice Chest* © Brenda Stewart. Pattern (intensive study booklet in alkyds and acrylics) available for $16.95.

PEGGY STOGDILL, MDA, PO Box 4653, Boynton Beach, FL 33424; phone: (561) 737-3694; fax: (561) 737-9693; p. 65 *Bountiful* © Peggy Stogdill. Pattern available for $16.00 plus $1.50 postage and handling. Send check or money order.

KIT STONER, CDA, 108 Alexander Lane, Lewistown, PA 17044; Voicemail: (717) 242-0897; fax: (717) 242-1993; e-mail: wls@acsworld.net; p. 113 *The Sea Captain* © Kit Stoner. Pattern available for $8 plus $2 shipping and handling. PA residents include 6% sales tax.

VI THURMOND, MDA, 343 S.E. Miller, Des Moines, IA 50315; phone: (515) 244-8061; fax: (515) 244-3880; p. 112 *Treasures* © Vi Thurmond. Pattern available for $7.00 plus $2.00 shipping and handling ($2.75 in Canada).

MARY JANE TODD, 636 Dogwood, Kuttawa, KY 42055; phone: (502) 388-7559; p. 56 *Red Bird in Fruit Bowl* © Mary Jane Todd. Pattern available for $7.50, including shipping and handling. Please request pattern packet 1070.

COLLEEN UNDERWOOD, CDA, 70 Woodward Crescent, Halifax, Nova Scotia, Canada B3M 1J7; phone/fax: (902) 443-7032; e-mail: Kaswood@ns.sympatico.ca; p. 36 *Mother's Roses* © Colleen Underwood. Pattern available for $10 plus $1 for postage.

PRUDY E. VANNIER, CDA, Prudy's Studio, Inc., 279 Maplewood St., Northville, MI 48167-1149; phone: (248) 380-0220; fax: (248) 380-0221; p. 57 *Pears* © Prudy E. Vannier. Pattern available for $5 plus $1 shipping and handling. Visa/MasterCard accepted. Send SASE for complete pattern listing.

PAT VIRCH, 1506 Lynn Ave., Marquette, MI 49855-1635; phone: (906) 226-3931; e-mail: virchinc@aol.com; pp. 8-9 *Company Coming Serving Plate* © Pat Virch, p. 117 *Telemark Tine* © Pat Virch, p. 125 *Telemark Bible Box* © Pat Virch. Full-size, color-coded patterns available for $4 each, prepaid with check or money order. No credit cards.

PAT WAKEFIELD, MDA, PO Box 3245, Shawnee Mission, KS 66203; phone: (931) 649-8318; e-mail: PJWake@aol.com; p. 13 *Iris Still Life* © Pat Wakefield. Catalog of publications available by request.

DONNA BRYANT WATERSON, Donna Bryant Publications, 3817 Cozy Drive, Wichita, KS 67220; phone: (316) 682-6867; fax: (316) 682-7114; pp. cover, 2, 31 *Roses* © Donna Bryant Waterson.

PAT WAYMON, PO Box 1429, Denison, TX 75021; phone: (903) 463-4090; fax: (903) 463-2006; p. 44 *Spring* © Pat Waymon. Pattern available for $8. Other pattern packets available by request.

LIN WELLFORD, Stone Menagerie/Rockcreations, Public Square Box 2,Green Forest, AR 72638; phone: (870) 438-5537; fax: (870) 438-6700; p. 100 *Tiger Rock* © Lin Wellford. Full color step-by-step instructions for this and many other rock creations can be found in Wellford's three North Light books, *The Art of Painting Animals on Rocks*, *Painting Houses, Cottages and Towns on Rocks* and *Painting More Animals on Rocks*.

DOROTHY WHISENHUNT, CDA, Art With Heart, PO Box 1781, Ruidoso, NM 88355-1781; phone: (505) 258-3297; p. 97 *Nestin' Instinct* © Dorothy Whisenhunt. Pattern available for $6.50. Includes four photos.

JOAN M. WILDING, CDA, 325 South Beacon St., Fall River, MA 02724; phone: (508) 678-8280; p. 63 *Fruits A' Plenty* © Joan M. Wilding. Pattern available for $9.50. Includes very detailed shading and highlighting information and detailed photos.

MARY M. WISEMAN, Marys Publications, 12856 Whitfield, Sterling Heights, MI 48312; phone: (810) 264-7328; p. 59 *Bread Box Fruit* © Mary M. Wiseman. Pattern available for $8.50 plus $1.50 shipping and handling.